THE CELTIC
BABY NAMES
BOOK

THE CELTIC BABY NAMES BOOK

Over 2,500 names

Compiled by
Gillian Delaforce

Vermilion
LONDON

1 3 5 7 9 10 8 6 4 2

First published in the United Kingdom in 2007 by Vermilion,
an imprint of Ebury Publishing
Random House UK Ltd.
Random House
20 Vauxhall Bridge Road
London SW1V 2SA

Random House Australia (Pty) Limited
20 Alfred Street, Milsons Point, Sydney,
New South Wales 2061, Australia

Random House New Zealand Limited
18 Poland Road, Glenfield,
Auckland 10, New Zealand

Random House (Pty) Limited
Isle of Houghton, Corner Boundary Road & Carse O'Gowrie
Houghton, 2198, South Africa

Random House Publishers India Private Limited
301 World Trade Tower, Hotel Intercontinental Grand Complex, Barakhamba Lane,
New Delhi 110 001, India

Random House UK Limited Reg. No. 954009
www.randomhouse.co.uk
Papers used by Vermilion are natural, recyclable products made from wood grown in
sustainable forests.

A CIP catalogue record is available for this book from the British Library.

ISBN: 9780091912703

Printed and bound in Great Britain by
Mackays of Chatham plc, Chatham, Kent

Contents

Introduction

One historian described the original Celtic tribes as 'indiscriminate barbarians'. However, the Greek historian Diodorus describes the Celts in vivid terms:

Their aspect is terrifying... They are very tall in stature, with rippling muscles under clear white skin. Their hair is blond, but not naturally so: they bleach it... artificially, washing it in lime and combing it back from their foreheads. They look like wood-demons, their hair thick and shaggy like a horse's mane. Some of them are clean-shaven, but others – especially those of high rank – shave their cheeks but leave a moustache that covers the whole mouth and, when they eat and drink, acts like a sieve, trapping particles of food... They wear brightly coloured and embroidered shirts, with trousers called 'bracae' and cloaks fastened at the shoulder with a brooch... These cloaks are striped or chequered in design, with the separate checks close together and in various colours.

They wear bronze helmets with figures picked out on them, even horns, which make them look even taller than they already are... while others cover themselves with the weapons nature gave them: they go naked into battle.

The Celtic tribes were called 'Galli' by the Romans, 'Galatai' in Asia Minor and 'Keltoi' by the Greeks, all terms meaning 'barbarian'. The word 'Celt' is derived from 'Keltoi'. In the third millennium BC, this ancient race dominated most of central Europe including southwest Germany, France (ancient Gaul) and eastwards along the river Danube. They had a common culture and language. In the seventh and sixth centuries BC, they made inroads into northern Iberia, which is the modern Basque country. They spread into Italy, as documented in Livy's *The Early History of Rome*, and sacked Rome in 390 BC. Delphi in Greece followed in 279 BC and Galatia, modern Turkey, in 276 BC. The 'La Tène' Iron-Age

Celts invaded Britain about 250 BC, although some Celtic tribes had been established there since 650 BC.

The first wave of Celtic immigrants to Britain, called the 'Q-Celts', spoke Goidelic and pronounced certain words with a 'k' sound. The later wave, referred to as 'P-Celts', spoke Brythonic and pronounced the same words with a 'p' sound. Goidelic led to the three Gaelic languages spoken in Ireland, the Isle of Man and, later, Scotland, while Brythonic formed the Cornish and Welsh languages, as well as the Breton spoken in French Brittany.

During the third to first centuries BC the Celtic tribes formed themselves into small kingdoms guarded by hill forts. The Kingdom of Scotia was founded in the Scottish Highlands. Some of the Celtic chieftains developed a taste for wine, and in their burial chambers Greek amphorae, tableware and drinking vessels have been found as well as swords, bracelets and mirrors.

Signs of Celtic farming – cultivated terraces called 'lynchets' – can still be seen in the downs of southeast England. Small gold mines were worked in Wales and the west of England.

As in most societies, there were social distinctions among the Celts. The warrior aristocrats were buried with silver vessels and other valuable possessions. Then came the freemen, cultivators of the land, the serfs and the slaves who were certainly not free, as can be seen by the chains and manacles that have survived in many burial sites.

Women played a prominent part in Celtic society and were warriors, powerful rulers and poets. However, there were many more male than female names and some have been used for both sexes.

The early Celtic religion was pagan and the Celts worshipped many gods and goddesses. There were Druidic ceremonies held in sacred groves by pools and lakes, and many of the old legends tell of the magical powers of the kings and princes and of the fairy people. In Scotland there are the magical tales of Oisín or Ossian and in Ireland of Cúchulainn and Conchobar and Saint Brigid and Deidre of the Sorrows.

One of the best-known legends is that of King Arthur and his Round Table. Many of the old Celtic names are those of the heroic knights who searched for the Holy Grail and of their beautiful ladies and the other nobles at his court. Also, there are tales of the wizard Merlin and other magicians with supernatural abilities who could change their shape at will.

The late Celtic period in Britain saw the birth of Christianity, which produced many saints whose names feature in this book. The Irish Saint Columba founded a religious community in Iona and sent missionaries to convert the Scots in the Highlands. Distinctive Celtic Christian art in the form of the *Lindisfarne Gospels* (c. 700), and the Irish *Book of Kells* from the same period, still survive. From Ireland to Iona and Lindisfarne, the early missionaries spread their faith and gave their names to churches and monasteries whose schools fostered learning and literature.

There is currently a huge resurgence of interest in genealogy and in searching out one's roots. People are keen to delve back to early civilisations from which family ancestors came, hence the fascination with all things Celtic and a pride in a shared background and culture.

The old names that came down through the oral tradition of story-telling have many variations of spelling as nothing was written down at the time, and may have been Latin, French, Irish or English. Celtic names often originate from nicknames associated with complexion or colouring, such as 'dark-haired', 'swarthy', 'ruddy-skinned' or 'golden-haired'. Frequently they are made up of two parts, as in the large number of Welsh names that end in 'gwen', meaning 'fair', 'good' or 'pure'.

The derivation of names is a very imprecise science. Similar-sounding Gaelic words may mean different things, hence various sources will give quite dissimilar meanings. This does not necessarily mean that one is right and one is wrong, just that there are different valid interpretations.

Enjoy looking through the plethora of unusual and traditional names given here. Whichever name you choose for your baby, you can be sure that it comes from one of the regions – Brittany, Cornwall, the Isle of Man, Ireland, Scotland or Wales – into which the Celts spread so long ago and where they have left their legacy.

A–Z OF
GIRLS' NAMES

A ~ Girls

Aalid
A Manx name that means 'beauty'.

Aalin
A Manx name meaning 'beautiful'.

Aalish
A Manx form of Alice.

Aamor
This Breton name appears to have some connection with the French for 'love'.
OTHER FORM: Aenor.

Aaue
The Manx equivalent of Eva.

Aderyn
A Welsh name meaning 'bird'.
OTHER FORM: Adarn.

Adigis
The name of the mother of the Cornish Saint Sererena.

Ado
A short form of the Cornish Gunoda.

Adwen
The patron saint of Cornish sweethearts, she was one of the daughters of a sixth-century king of Powys.

Aebbe
An early abbess who founded a mixed-community monastery at Saint Abbs.

Aedh
Comes from the Gaelic for 'fire'.

Aela
Feminine form of Ael, the name of an early Breton saint.

Aelid
A name used on the Isle of Man, which means 'beauty'.

Aelwen
This means 'fair brow' in Welsh, but is also found in Brittany and Cornwall.

Aerona
Taken from the Welsh for 'like a berry'.

Aeronwen

This Welsh name means 'white' or 'blessed'.

Africa

Possibly derived from the Gaelic for 'speckled', this was a popular name in 12th-century Scotland and in the Isle of Man.

OTHER FORMS: Afreka, Aifric, Eafric.

Africah

The name of a 12th-century queen of the Isle of Man.

Afton

The name of a Scottish river.

Agrona

In Welsh mythology the River Aeron, which washes the arms of warriors before battle, is named after her.

Aibhlinn

A name taken to Ireland by the Normans.

Aibreán

An Irish name derived from the Gaelic for April.

Aideen

Taken from the Gaelic meaning 'fire', implying someone with red hair.

Aigneas

A Gaelic version of Agnes.

Aígréne

This means 'ray of sunshine' and was the name of the daughter of Deidre and Naoise.

Aileas

The Gaelic version of Alice.

Aileen

A name used in the Isle of Man, which is the equivalent of Helen.

OTHER FORMS: Aila, Ailene.

Ailie

A Gaelic version of Alison.

Ailinn

A doomed lover who, when she heard of her lover's death, died of grief and an apple tree grew from her grave.

Ailis

An Irish form of Alice.

Ailish

An Irish version of Alice.

Ailsa

The name of an island in Scotland, which is used as a girl's name but formerly would also have been masculine.

OTHER FORM: Elsa.

Ailstreena

The female form of Alistair, used on the Isle of Man.

Aimel

A Manx name that means 'beloved'.

OTHER FORM: Emell.

Aine

The name of an ancient Irish goddess, meaning 'brilliance'.

Aingeal

The Gaelic equivalent of 'angel'.

Ainle

A Manx name meaning 'an angel'.

Ainslie

This name originated in Scotland and probably means 'one meadow'.

OTHER FORM: Ainslie.

Airmid

She was the daughter of Diancécht, the Irish god of medicine.

Aisline

From the Gaelic for 'dream' or 'vision'.

OTHER FORM: Aisling.

Aithne

Meaning 'little fire', this is popular in Ireland and was the name of a goddess and various queens and saints.

Alana

To be found in Scotland, this is the feminine form of Alan.

OTHER FORMS: Allanah, Lana.

Alaw

This means 'melody' in Welsh.

Aleine

In the Arthurian legends, she was the niece of Sir Gawain.

Alienor

A Breton version of Eleanor.

Alina

Connected to the Gaelic for 'lovely'.

Alis

A Welsh name borne by an early poet.

Alistreena

The Manx feminine form of Alistair.

Allasan
A Scottish Gaelic version of Alison.

Almeda
This Breton name may have been derived from the word for 'soul'.

Almha
The name of an Irish goddess who had great strength.
OTHER FORMS: Alva, Alvag.

Amaethon
A goddess of agriculture.

Amena
'Pure' or 'honest'.
OTHER FORMS: Amina, Amine.

Anabal
The Gaelic version of Annabel.

Anchoret
From the Welsh for 'much loved'.

Andrea
A feminine form of Andrew.

Andreca
The Manx feminine form of Andrew.

Aneira
From the Welsh 'truly white' or 'snow'.

Anest
From the Welsh for 'honour'.

Angharad
A Welsh princess, she is mentioned several times in the early chronicles.
OTHER FORM: Ancret.

Angusina
The feminine form of Angus.

Annes
A variation of Agnes.

Annowre
She tried to steal the sword Excalibur when King Arthur did not respond to her love.

Anta
A fifth-century missionary saint who founded a religious house in Cornwall.

Anu
A variation of Danu, the mother goddess of the Celts.

Anwen
Welsh for 'very fair'.

Aobh
From the Gaelic for 'beauty' and is thought to equate to the first woman, Eve.

Aodhnait

A female version of Aodh, meaning 'fire'.

Aoibheann

An old Irish Gaelic name that can be translated as 'radiance'.
OTHER FORMS: Aoibhinn, Aoibhnait.

Aoibhel

In Irish myths she was a harpist whose beautiful music caused any listener to die in ecstasy.

Aoife

A fierce female warrior in Irish myths, whose name means 'radiant'.
OTHER FORM: Ava.

Aouregwern

This Breton name has similar roots to the Welsh for 'white' or 'fair'.

Aourkan

In ninth-century Brittany, it was recorded that a woman of this name held a high political position.

Arabella

A medieval Scottish name.

Aranrhod

A Welsh goddess of the dawn.
OTHER FORM: Arianrod.

Ardanata

In Welsh myths she was described as a beautiful woman.

Arddun

From the Welsh for 'beautiful'.

Argante

Goddess of the Underworld in Celtic myths.

Arianwen

From the Welsh meaning 'silvery'.
OTHER FORMS: Aranwen, Arwenna.

Arlena

This is possibly derived from the Gaelic for 'pledge'.
FRENCH FORM: Arlène.

Armelle

In Brittany, this is a name thought to mean 'of high rank'.

Athracht

A sixth-century Irish saint.
OTHER FORM: Attracta.

Aude

The name of a Cornish saint who was martyred in the 11th century and also of a Breton princess.

Aufrica

A popular name among the Manx from early Christian times, which means a maid from Africa.

Aurick

This name from the Isle of Man means a 'maid from Africa'.

OTHER FORM: **Averick**.

Awel

From the Welsh for 'breeze'.

Awen

Meaning 'the muse' in Welsh.

Awena

The Welsh for 'poetry'.

Azenor

The mother of a Breton saint who became bishop of Dol.

B ~ Girls

Badb
One of the triune goddesses, her name was synonymous with rage or frenzy.

Bahee
A pet form of Margaret used in the Isle of Man.

Bahy
A Manx name meaning 'flower'.

Báibre
The Irish form of Barbara.
OTHER FORM: Baibín.

Banba
An ancient poetic name for the Isle of Man.

Barabal
The Gaelic version of Barbara.

Beara
A legendary Celtic princess whose love for her husband broke the spell that had turned him into a fish.

Bearnas
The Gaelic version of Berenice.

Beatha
Probably from the Gaelic word for 'life'.
OTHER FORMS: Beata, Bethia.

Beathag
The feminine form of Beathan, meaning 'offspring of life'.

Bec
From the Gaelic for 'small'.

Becca
Another form of Bec or a diminutive of Rebecca.

Becuma
In Irish myths she married Conn of the Hundred Battles.

Begga
An early Celtic saint who was married to another saint, Arnulf of Metz.

Béibhinn

The name of 11th-century Irish princesses, this means 'fair lady'.

Beithris

The Gaelic version of Beatrice.

Benalban

This means 'lady from Scotland'.

Benally

This means 'Ulster woman'.

Benvon

This means 'lady from Munster'.

Benvy

This means 'lady from Meath'.

Beoferlic

The Celtic version of Beverley. This was the name of a woman priest and bishop in the sixth century.

Berched

The Breton form of Brid.

Berneen

An Irish form of Bernadette.

Beryan

The name of a Cornish saint.
OTHER FORM: Beriana.

Beth

May derive from the Scottish Gaelic word for 'life', as Macbeth means 'son of life'.
OTHER FORM: Betha.

Bethan

This Welsh name may be derived from the word for 'life'.
OTHER FORM: Bethen.

Beti

The Welsh version of Betty.

Betrys

The Welsh version of Beatrice.

Betsan

The Welsh version of Betsy.

Bevin

A more modern version of the Irish Béibhinn.

Bia

The name of an early abbess in County Armagh, Ireland.

Biddy

A pet form of Brigid, this name was once common in Ireland but now is linked with someone who is a tiresome old woman.
OTHER FORMS: Bidelia, Bedelia.

Bíle

The name of a sacred oak tree in Welsh mythology.

OTHER FORM: Beli.

Biróg

A mythical female druid in Irish mythology.

Blaa

A Manx name that means 'flower'.

OTHER FORM: Blae.

Blaine

Probably comes from the Gaelic for 'narrow'.

OTHER FORM: Blayne.

Blair

A Scottish name derived from the Gaelic 'from the field'.

Bláithín

This can be anglicised as Blossom as it is derived from the Gaelic for 'flower'.

Blanaid

One of the names that come from the Gaelic for 'flower'.

Blathnát

A name meaning 'little flower'.

Blejan

A Cornish name meaning 'flower' or 'bloom'.

Blinne

The sixth-century Irish saint of this name was friendly with Saint Patrick and Saint Brigid.

OTHER FORM: Bluinse.

Blodeuwydd

The legend has it that she was turned into an owl because she was unfaithful. In Welsh the name means 'flower aspect'.

Blodwen

A Welsh name meaning 'white flower'.

OTHER FORM: Blodeyn.

Boann

The river Boyne was named after the goddess who bore this name.

Bonnie

A Scottish name which means 'fair'.

OTHER FORM: Bonny.

Boudicca

First-century queen of the Iceni who successfully fought the Romans when they invaded Celtic Britain but was eventually captured and committed suicide.

LATINISED FORM: Boadicea.

Brangaine

In Celtic legends she was Isolda's maid.

Branna

Probably derived from the Gaelic for 'raven'.

Branwen

A mythological Irish queen, she died of a broken heart.

OTHER FORM: Brangwen.

Breaca

A fifth-century Irish missionary to Cornwall.

Breage

Cornish patron saint of midwives.

OTHER FORM: Breagg.

Bree

Means 'exalted' and can also be a version of Bríd.

Breege

An Irish name pronounced the same way as Bríd.

Breesha

An old Manx form of Bridey.

OTHER FORM: Breeshey.

Breifne

A fierce female warrior in Irish sagas.

Brenda

The Vikings brought this name to the Shetlands and it was adopted by the Scots.

Brengain

The Welsh form of Brenda.

Brenna

The female form of Brennan, probably meaning 'sorrow' or 'tear'.

Bretna

An old Manx name meaning 'a maid from Britain'.

Briallen

Derived from the Welsh word for 'primrose'.

Brianna

The Welsh female form of Brian.

OTHER FORM: Brianne.

Bríd

A variation of Brigid and a name frequently found in Ireland.

OTHER FORM: Bree.

Bridget
An anglicised form of Brigid.

Bridie
A very popular Irish name derived from
Brigid.
OTHER FORMS: Bride, Brede, Bridey.

Brighde
A Gaelic version of Bridget.

Brigid
This means 'exalted one'. She is the
mother goddess and the goddess of
fertility.
OTHER FORMS: Brigit, Brigitta.

Brígnat
The name of an early Irish nun.

Brisen
A magician at the court of King Arthur.

Britannia
A British Celtic image of motherland.

Brittany
The English name for a region of
western France, which comes from a
Celtic root.
OTHER FORM: Brittney.

Broiseach
Reputedly the mother of Brigid of Kildare.

Brollachan
This magical female spirit is said to
inhabit the north of Scotland and can
change her shape at will.

Brónach
Gaelic for 'sorrowful'.
OTHER FORM: Brona.

Bronwen
From the Welsh for 'white breast', this is
a very popular name in Wales.
OTHER FORMS: Brongwyn, Bronwyn,
Oronwen.

Bryana
'Noble' or 'virtuous'.

Bryna
The female form of the Welsh Bryn,
meaning 'hill'.

Bryony
Possibly derived from the Welsh for 'hill'
or taken from the name of the wild
flower.

Buádnat

A female warrior known as 'victorious lady' in the old Irish sagas.

Buan

One of Cúchulainn's mistresses, who died when trying to jump onto his chariot.

Búanann

Known as the 'mother of heroes' in Irish myths, a woman of this name ran a martial arts academy.

Buchat

Legend has it that her cow was abducted by a magic bull.

Buí

The Irish for 'yellow'.

Buryan

The name of a fifth-century Irish missionary to Cornwall.

C ~ Girls

Cáelinn
An Irish name that means 'fair and slender'.

Caera
From the Gaelic for 'spear-like'.
OTHER FORM: Ceara.

Caeribormeith
The name of a goddess who could change her shape at will and spent half her life as a swan.

Cailleach
The wife of the god Lugh Lámhfada, she had seven husbands and 50 foster children.

Cairenn
In Irish myths she was the second wife of Eochaidh and mother of Niall of the Nine Hostages.
OTHER FORM: Karen.

Cairistiona
A Scottish name derived from the Gaelic for 'a Christian'.

Caitlin
The Celtic form of Katherine.
OTHER FORMS: Kaitlin, Kaytlin.

Caitrin
An Irish Gaelic form of Catherine.

Caja
A Cornish name meaning 'daisy'.

Caly
A Manx name for a female servant.

Calybride
This means 'Saint Bridget's servant'.

Calycrist
A Manx name meaning 'servant of Christ'.

Calyhony
A Manx name that means 'Saint Oney's servant'.

Calyree
A Manx name that means 'the king's servant'.

Calyvorra

A Manx name that means 'St Mary's servant'.

Camma

Plutarch has a story about this priestess of the goddess Brigid who poisoned the man who had killed her husband and had forced her to marry him.

Camryn

A feminine version of Cameron.

Caoilfhinn

This Irish name comes from the Gaelic for 'fair and slender'.

Caoimhe

This has many meanings, such as 'precious' and 'graceful'.

Cara

A traditional Manx name meaning 'songster'.

Caragh

A version of Cara found in Ireland.

Carainn

The Irish version of Karen.

Carmán

The name of the legendary mother of three fierce warriors.

Carola

A traditional Manx name meaning 'noble spirited'.
OTHER FORM: Kavel.

Caronwyn

Derived from the Welsh for 'fair' and 'beloved'.

Carree

A Manx name meaning 'music'.

Cartimandua

A powerful queen of the early Britons, her name means 'sleek pony'.

Caryl

In Welsh this has the connotation of 'beloved'.

Caryn

A variation of Karin.

Cathbad

A druidess, she prophesied that Deidre would be the fairest woman in all Ireland but that only sorrow would come from her beauty.

Cathbodua

This was the name of a Celtic goddess of war.

Cathleen

A variation of Kathleen.

OTHER FORM: Cathline.

Catreena

A Manx form of Catherine.

Catrin

There were two early Welsh poetesses of this name.

Catriona

This means 'pure' and became popular due to Robert Louis Stevenson's book of the same name.

OTHER FORMS: Caitriona, Catrina, Katrina, Triona.

Ceasg

In Scottish myths this was the name for beautiful mermaids.

Ceindrych

Welsh for 'an elegant sight'.

Ceinlys

A Welsh name that means 'jewels'.

Ceinwen

From the Welsh for 'blessed' or 'white'.

Ceiros

The Welsh word for 'cherries'.

Ceri

A popular name in Wales, from the Welsh for 'love'.

OTHER FORMS: Cari, Carys, Ceris, Cerys.

Cerian

This means 'to love' in Welsh.

OTHER FORM: Ceril.

Ceridwen

A Celtic goddess, mother of the poet, Taliesin.

OTHER FORM: Ceiridwen.

Cerwyn

This is used for boys as well as girls and means 'fair love' in Welsh.

Cessair

The story is told that she was so unhappy when her husband died that she died of grief soon after him. In sympathy, the heavens opened and all of Ireland was flooded.

Charlotte

The wife of James I of Man came from a Breton family, and when he was defeated and executed by Charles II she became legally 'Lord of Man'.

Chesten

An old Cornish form of Christine.

Chevonne

A variation of Siobhan.

Chiendeg

Means 'elegant' or 'fair' in Welsh.

Chiomara

A queen of the Galatian Celts who led her people against the Romans.

Ciara

The feminine form of Ciaran, this comes from the word meaning 'dark' or 'dark brown'.
OTHER FORM: Keera.

Cigfa

In the Celtic sagas she was the wife of a king of Dyfed. The name may derive from the Welsh for 'raven'.

Ciorstaidh

A Gaelic version of Christina.

Cissolt

A Manx name meaning 'little Cecilia'.

Clarisant

In the Arthurian legends she was the sister of Sir Gawain.

Climidh

A Gaelic version of Clementine.

Clíodhna

A fairy woman in Irish legends.
OTHER FORMS: Cleona, Cliona.

Clodagh

From the name of a river in Tipperary, Ireland.
OTHER FORM: Claudia.

Clothra

The ambitious sister of the legendary Queen Medb.

Cody

Originally a surname, Mac Oda, this is now used occasionally for girls.
OTHER FORMS: Codi, Kody.

Coinchend

One of the tough female warriors in Irish mythology.

Colleen

The Irish word for 'girl', which was often used in other countries as a generic term for an Irish girl.

OTHER FORM: Colene.

Columba

More commonly known as a male saint, this was also the name of a Cornish female saint who lived in the fourth century.

Conla

The female version of Conal, a Manx name meaning 'love'.

Cora

In Ireland this is a female form of Corey.

OTHER FORM: Coralie.

Cordelia

Shakespeare used this Celtic name in his play *King Lear* and it is possible that it means 'harmony'.

OTHER FORM: Creuddylad.

Cori

An Irish female form of Corey.

Cossot

A Manx diminutive of Constance.

Creana

A Manx name meaning 'wise'.

Créd

There are several women in Irish history with this name but the most famous was married to an elderly chief. There are many romantic tales of her love for a prince who came from Skye.

Creda

A saintly woman in the sixth century who was the mother of the second abbot of Iona.

Credha

A female warrior in Irish sagas.

Creed

A female missionary in sixth-century Cornwall.

OTHER FORM: Crida.

Creena

A Manx name meaning 'wise' or 'prudent'.

Creiddylad

This old Celtic name has no definite meaning but it might be related to the Welsh for 'heron'.

Creidne

In the Irish sagas she learnt martial arts and was a relentless warrior of the Fianna.

Creirwy

A Welsh name that may mean 'fair heron'.

Crera

A Manx name meaning 'faithful'.

Creuddylad

The Welsh form of Cordelia.

Crewenna

A Cornish name borne by a saint from Crowab.

Crisiant

Probably derived from the Welsh for 'crystal'.

Cristina

Prioress of the only abbey on the Isle of Man in the 15th century.
OTHER FORM: Cristeena.

Cristory

A Manx name meaning 'of Christ'.

Crowan

An early Christian missionary who founded a church in Cornwall.

Crystabel

This name appears in medieval legends, where she discovered just in time that she was going to marry her own son.

Crystal

Although the name of a semi-precious stone, this could also be a shortened form of Crystabel.

Crystyn

In Wales this is found as a form of Christine.

Cushla

An Irish term of endearment meaning 'beat of my heart'.

Cyhyreith

The Welsh equivalent of the Irish 'fairy woman'.

Cymidia

The legendary goddess of war, healing and procreation. She was reputed to give birth to a fully armed warrior every six weeks.
OTHER FORM: Cymidei.

D ~ Girls

Dacey
A name derived from the Gaelic for 'from the south'.

Dahud
The daughter of a king of Brittany, who rebelled against the advent of Christianity.

Dáiligh
A transferred surname that means 'meeting'.
OTHER FORM: Daley.

Daimhín
An Irish name from the Gaelic for 'little deer'.

Dairine
In Irish myths she was married to the same man as her sister at the same time, and both girls died of shame because of it.
OTHER FORM: Darina.

Dalys
From the Irish Gaelic meaning 'wise'.

Damnhait
An Irish name that occurs throughout history, meaning 'fawn'.

Danu
The mother goddess of the Celts. This name is the origin of many river names such as the Danube.
OTHER FORMS: Anu, Dana, Dane, Dayna.

Dara
Derived from the Gaelic for 'oak'.
OTHER FORM: Deri.

Darby
An Irish name, which might mean 'free'.

Darcey
A transferred Irish surname which means 'descended from the dark one'.

Darerca
Several missionaries and teachers of the early Christian church bore this name, which means 'daughter of Erc'.

Darfhinn

This Irish princess was the wife of a king of Leinster, and the name is derived from the Gaelic for 'fair daughter'.

Darlughdacha

This means 'daughter of the sun god Lugh'. She was Brigid's successor as abbess of Kildare.

Darran

Although often used as a boy's name, this feminine form is derived from the Gaelic word that means 'oak'.

Davina

A Scottish feminine form of David.

Dearbhail

This is an old Irish name, taken from the Gaelic for 'daughter of Fal' (a poetic name for Ireland).

Dechtire

The mother of Cúchulainn.

Dee

Possibly derived from the River Dee in Scotland. It is also a short form for all names beginning with the letter D.

Deirbhile

The name of a sixth-century Irish saint, this means 'daughter of the poet'.

Deirdre

A tragic heroine in Celtic history, known as 'Deirdre of the Sorrows'.
OTHER FORMS: Deidra, Deirdriú.

Delbchaem

In Irish myths she was the wife of Art, a high king of Ireland.

Delwyn

Derived from the Welsh for 'fair' and 'pretty'.

Delyth

The Welsh for 'pretty'.

Demelza

The name of a place in Cornwall.

Derlasra

The name of an abbess of Killeavy Abbey during the first century of Christianity.

Derryth

This Welsh name is derived from the words for 'oak' and 'Druid'.

Dervla

The anglicised form of Deirbhile, meaning 'daughter of the poet'.

OTHER FORM: Dervila.

Devorgilla

A name that means 'daughter of Forgal', which appears in history and legends.

Dilecq

The Breton form of Dilic.

Dilic

The name of an early Cornish saint.

OTHER FORM: Dilecq.

Dilie

Possibly a variation of Dilic or the name may have been borne by another Cornish saint.

Dilly

An affectionate form of Dilys.

Dilys

From the Welsh, meaning 'perfect' or 'true'.

OTHER FORM: Dilly.

Dindrane

In the Arthurian legends this was the name of Sir Percival's sister.

Diorval

A Manx name meaning 'true oath'.

Dogmaela

A female version of Dogmael, a Breton saint.

OTHER FORM: Dogmeela.

Domhnacha

An Irish version of Dominica and probably means 'the Lord's day'.

Dominica

Saint Dominica had a church dedicated to her in Cornwall in the 13th century.

Domnu

An Irish name that means 'the world' and is also the name of a goddess.

Dôn

Another name for Danu, the mother goddess of the Celts.

Donalda

In Scotland this is the female form of Donald.

Donna

This can be said to be a Celtic name as it could be derived from the Gaelic word that means 'noble'.

Doona

A Manx name meaning 'dark maiden'.

Dorwenna

Another name for the patron saint of lovers.

Douglasina

In Scotland this is a rare name, the feminine of Douglas.

Drema

A Manx name meaning 'someone who tries hard'.

Drudwen

Welsh for 'precious'.

Drusa

An old name that may be connected to the Gaelic for 'druid'.

Dryadia

Dryades were druidesses in early Celtic times.

Duana

A feminine form of Duane, which comes from the Gaelic for 'dark-haired'.

Dubh

This is derived from the Gaelic for 'dark'. Dublin was named after a druidess called Dubh.

Duinead

The Irish for 'strong'.

Dwyn

The patron saint of lovers but never married.
OTHER FORM: Dwynwen.

Dyfr

One of the 'Three Splendid Maidens' of King Arthur's court, she was renowned for her golden-haired beauty.

Dymphna

There was an early saint of this name and there is a shrine dedicated to her in Belgium.

E ~ Girls

Eabha
A fierce female warrior who wound iron bars into her long red hair to make herself more frightening.

Eachna
She was supposed to be the most beautiful and wise woman in the world.

Eadain
A variation of Étain.

Ealasaid
A Gaelic version of Elizabeth.

Ealee
A Manx name meaning 'noble'.

Ealga
From the Gaelic for 'noble', this is part of an old poetic name for Ireland, 'Innis Ealga'.

Ealisaid
A Manx name meaning 'God's oath'.

Ealish
A Manx form of Alice.

Eamag
The Gaelic version of Emily.

Eamair
One of the variations of the name of Cúchulainn's wife.

Eamnhait
In the ninth century a woman of this name was rescued from a snowdrift with her baby and given succour by some monks.

Eapag
The Gaelic version of Euphemia.

Eavan
An anglicised version of Aoibhinn, which means 'attractive'.

Ebrel
The Cornish form of April.

Ecca

A name from Irish myths.

Edana

From the Gaelic for 'fiery', this is a female form of the Irish name Edan.

Edme

The Scottish form of Esmé.

Effrddyl

An early Welsh saintly woman.

Effric

A Gaelic version of Africa.

Effrica

This means a 'maid from Africa'.

Egidia

An aristocratic Manx name.

Eibhlin

The name of one of the most famous Irish women poets in the 18th century.

Eibhlis

One of the Irish versions of Alice.

Eigr

In the Arthurian legends she was the mother of King Arthur.

Eileen

Originally an Irish name, there are many poems about her with lines such as 'sweet Eileen from Erin's green shore'.

Eilidh

A Gaelic version of Helen.

Eilir

This Welsh name means 'butterfly' or 'spring'.

Eilis

An Irish version of Alice.
OTHER FORM: Eillish.

Eilispidh

A Gaelic version of Elizabeth.

Eiluned

This Welsh name is derived from the word for 'icon' or 'idol'.
OTHER FORMS: Eluned, Linet.

Eilwen

A Welsh name that means 'fair browed'.

Einín

From the Gaelic, this means 'little bird'.
OTHER FORM: Eneen.

Eira
From the Welsh word meaning 'snow'.

Eire
An ancient poetic name for the Isle of Man and also the name of a goddess who gave her name to Ireland.
OTHER FORMS: Erina, Eriu.

Eireann
This is probably a blend of Eire and Ann.
OTHER FORM: Eireen.

Eirian
A Welsh name meaning 'silver' or 'bright'.

Eirlys
From the Welsh for 'snowdrop'.

Eirwen
This Welsh name is made up of the words for 'snow' and 'white'.

Eithne
One of the early Celtic saints or goddesses, this ancient name is experiencing a revival.
OTHER FORMS: Eithna, Ethniu.

Elen
In the fourth century a British chieftain's daughter of this name married a Roman emperor called Magnus who ruled Britain, Gaul and Iberia.

Elena
The Manx version of Helena.
OTHER FORM: Eilleen.

Eleri
This is an old Welsh name of unknown origin.

Elis
A Welsh form of Alice.

Elowen
A Cornish name that means 'elm'.

Elspeth
A Scottish version of Elizabeth.
OTHER FORMS: Elsie, Elspie.

Elspie
A pet form of Elspeth.

Elwa
Taken from the Welsh for 'benefit'.
OTHER FORM: Elwy.

Emer

The name of the wife of Cúchulainn, who forgave him for his numerous affairs.

OTHER FORM: Eimhir.

Ena

Probably derived from the Gaelic for 'little fire'.

OTHER FORMS: Edna, Enya.

Enat

May be derived from the Welsh for 'soul' and is the feminine form of Aidan.

Enda

Although there was a monk in the sixth century who bore this name, it is also given to girls.

Endelienta

A female missionary in sixth-century Cornwall.

Endellion

Related to the Welsh for 'soul' and the Irish for 'fire', this was the name of an early saint.

Eneda

The name of a Cornish saint.

Enid

Derived from the Welsh for 'life' or 'soul', this name was used by Tennyson in his poetry.

OTHER FORM: Enida.

Epona

This legendary goddess was said to take brave warriors on her horse to paradise if they died fighting.

Erin

A poetic name for Ireland, which is used for both girls and boys.

Ertha

This name comes from Cornwall, where she was known as a saint.

OTHER FORM: Eartha.

Erwanez

A Breton name, this is probably a version of the Welsh Erwan.

Eseld

The Cornish form of Iseult.

Essa

A Manx name meaning 'of Jesus'.

Esyllt

The names of two women at King Arthur's court, this means 'white' or 'slender neck'.

Étain

There were many women of this name in the early history of Ireland and it is synonymous with the ideal Celtic beauty. In the legends she was magically changed into a fly which flew into a glass of water drunk by a barren woman who later gave birth to a beautiful daughter.

OTHER FORMS: Eadain, Etan.

Ethlin

The daughter of a mythical Irish ruler who was imprisoned in a crystal tower.

Ethna

She was reputed to exist only by drinking the milk of magic cows in order to be as pure as possible.

Ethné

The name of the mythical Queen Medb's sister, who was drowned by another sister when she was pregnant.

Eubonia

A popular name on the Isle of Man in the 18th century.

Eulalia

Well over a thousand years ago this name was recorded as being that of a Cornish martyr.

Euna

A Scottish version of Juno.

Eunys

This Manx name means 'joy' or 'ecstasy'.

Eurielle

A name that means 'angelic'.

Eurwen

Taken from the Welsh for 'gold' and 'fair'.

Ewe

The name of a female missionary in sixth-century Cornwall.

F ~ Girls

Fachanan
This probably comes from the Gaelic for 'hostile'. In the sixth or seventh century, Saint Fachanan established a learned community in Cork, Ireland.
OTHER FORM: Fachtna.

Faenche
A saint and the sister of the abbot, Saint Enda of Aran.

Fáinne
This is the Irish for 'ring' and has only relatively recently been used as a first name.

Falair
A Gaelic version of Hilary.

Falga
An ancient poetic name for the Isle of Man.

Fallon
Originally an Irish surname, this has recently become popular due to its use in soap operas.

Fanch
The Breton version of Francis, sometimes used for girls.

Fand
This means the 'pearl of beauty', and in the myths she was the wife of the sea god, Manannan.

Fay
A name which in Ireland has the connotation of someone who is somewhat 'otherworldly' and is also linked to 'faith'.

Feena
A Manx name meaning 'fair maiden'.

Feenat
Derived from the Gaelic for 'wild creature'.

Fenella
A variation of the Manx name, Finola.

Ferelith

This Scottish name is thought to mean 'perfect princess'.

Ffion

From the Welsh for 'foxglove', this is a poetic word meaning the cheek of a beautiful girl.

Fflur

The Welsh for flower.

Ffraid

In Wales, Saint Brigid was translated as Saint Ffraid.

Ffransis

The Welsh version of Frances.

Fianat

A name meaning 'little deer'.
OTHER FORM: Fiadhnaid.

Fianna

This comes from the name of the king's bodyguard under Finn Mac Cool, some of whom were probably women.

Fidelma

This may come from the Gaelic for 'constancy' and has been borne by many Celtic saints.
OTHER FORM: Fedelma.

Findabair

The daughter of the mythical king and queen, Medb and Ailill, her name means 'fair eyebrows'. In the old legends her lover fought for her hand in marriage and when he was killed she died of grief.
OTHER FORMS: Findbhair, Fionnabhair.

Fingola

This means 'fair shoulder' and comes from the Isle of Man.

Finna

From the Gaelic for 'white'.

Finnleacht

A princess of Meath who was regarded as a 'saint', her feast day in October is still celebrated.

Fiona

This Scots name is derived from the Gaelic meaning 'fair' or 'white'.
SHORT FORM: Fi.

Fionnabhair

A version of Findabair, this could mean 'sprite'.
OTHER FORM: Fionnúir.

Fionnaghul

A Gaelic equivalent of Fenella.

Fionnghal

Fionnghal Ní Dhòmhnuil was the real Celtic name of Flora Macdonald.

Fionnghuala

On the Isle of Man this name became Fingola.

Fionnuala

In Irish legend she and her three brothers were turned into swans and wandered the lakes and rivers until Christianity came to Ireland.
OTHER FORMS: Finola, Fionola, Fionula, Nola, Nuala.

Fírinne

This Irish name comes from the Gaelic word for 'verity' or 'truth'.

Fithir

The wife of a king in Irish myths.

Flaitheas

A goddess and patron of the O'Neill family, whose name means 'sovereignty'.

Flanna

A feminine form of Flann, which means 'blood red'.

Floraidh

The Gaelic version of Flora.

Floreans

The Gaelic version of Florence.

Fótla

A poetic name for Ireland, and also of one of the three goddesses of sovereignty.
OTHER FORM: Fodla.

Francaig

A Manx version of Frances.

Frangag

A Gaelic version of Frances.

Frann

This may be derived from the Gaelic for 'sea bird'.

Franseza

A Breton version of Frances.

Freya

A name brought to Shetland and then Scotland by the Norwegians.

Fritha

A Manx name that means 'peace'.

Fuamnach

In the legends, when her husband took a younger wife, she wreaked her revenge by transforming the new wife into a fly.

G ~ Girls

Gael
Someone who speaks Gaelic and comes from one of the Celtic countries.
OTHER FORMS: Gaelle, Gail.

Gaenor
A Welsh version of Gaynor.

Gáine
The name of one of the chief druidesses of Ireland in early stories.

Ganeida
The name of the sorcerer Merlin's sister and also an alternative version of Gwendydd.

Ganna
A female prophet, her name probably means 'intermediary'.

Garwen
The name of one of King Arthur's mistresses.

Gaynor
An anglicised form of Guinevere, King Arthur's legendary queen.
OTHER FORM: Gaenor.

Gearóidin
The Irish version of Geraldine.

Gethan
A Welsh name derived from a nickname for someone who is dark-skinned.
OTHER FORM: Gethen.

Gilda
Derived from the Gaelic for 'servant of God'.

Gilfaethwy
The name of a Celtic goddess.

Giolla
The name of a famous 13th-century Ulster poet.

Giorsal
The Gaelic version of Grace.

Gladez

The Breton form of Gladys.

Gladys

The anglicised version of the Welsh Gwladys, which means 'ruler'.
OTHER FORMS: Glad, Gladez, Gladuse.

Glain

Derived from the Welsh for 'jewel'.

Glenda

A Welsh name meaning either 'purity' or 'girl from the valley'.
OTHER FORM: Glenna.

Glenn

One of the oldest known names, implying a girl from the glen.

Glesni

Derived from the Welsh for 'blue sky'.

Glyna

A female version of Glyn.

Glynis

From the Welsh for 'vale', this implies a girl who comes from the valley.
OTHER FORMS: Glenice, Glenys.

Glynne

A female form of Glyn or Glen.

Gobnet

Saint Gobnet founded several monasteries in County Cork, Ireland, and is the patron saint of beekeepers.
OTHER FORM: Gobnait.

Goewin

In the myths she was a virgin who was the foot-holder to Math and later married him.

Gofannon

The goddess of smith craft.

Goleuddydd

A name from Welsh myths, meaning 'daylight'.

Gormflaith

An outstanding poet of 10th-century Ireland, she was a queen who was married to three kings.
OTHER FORM: Gormla.

Gráinne

The legendary Irish princess, betrothed to Finn, who eloped with Dermot and killed herself after Finn brought about Dermot's death.
OTHER FORM: Grania.

Granuaile
A notable Irish female pirate in the 16th century who preyed on English ships.

Grayse
A Manx name that means 'grace'.

Grear
Derived from the Scots Gaelic for 'watchful'.

Greeba
The name of a mountain and a castle on the Isle of Man.

Gruoch
A Scottish queen, the original Lady Macbeth.

Guinevere
The wife of King Arthur who was loved by Launcelot of the legendary Knights of the Round Table.

Gulval
A female missionary in sixth-century Cornwall.
OTHER FORM: Wovela.

Gunoda
The name of a Cornish martyr, meaning 'blessed'.
SHORT FORM: Ado.

Gwenda
From the Welsh for 'fair' and 'good'.

Gwendolen
The Welsh for 'white ring', this probably refers to the legendary moon goddess.
OTHER FORMS: Gwen, Gwendolyn.

Gwendolena
The name of the magician Merlin's wife.

Gwendydd
In early Welsh tales she was the mother or sister of Myrddin Emrys.

Gweneira
Derived from the Welsh for 'pure' and 'snow'.

Gwenfrewi
The name of an early seventh-century Welsh saint.

Gwengualch
This early name means 'white falcon'.

Gwenhwyfar
The Welsh equivalent of Guinevere.

Gwenllian
The name of the sister of the last independent king of Wales.

Gwenna
A Breton form of Gwynne.

Gwennaig
One of the Breton versions of Gwynne.

Gwenonwyn
A Welsh name that means 'lily of the valley'.

Gwerful
A 15th-century Welsh poet, some of whose poems still survive.

Gwladus
The name of a sixth-century saint from Wales. There was also a Cornish Saint Gwladus.

Gwydian
The goddess of science and light.

Gwyl
The name of one of King Arthur's mistresses.

Gwynedd
The name of a Welsh county, this may come from the word for 'bliss'.

Gwyneth
A more modern version of Gwynedd.
OTHER FORMS: Gwyn, Gwenyth.

Gwynne
From the Welsh for 'fair' or 'pure'.
OTHER FORMS: Gwenna, Gwennaig.

H ~ Girls

Haf
From the Welsh for 'summer'.
OTHER FORM: Hafina.

Hafryn
Welsh name for the River Severn.

Hafwen
Welsh name meaning 'fair summer'.
OTHER FORM: Hafwyn.

Haley
May be derived from the Gaelic, meaning 'escape'.

Haude
This name from Brittany is probably related to the Breton name Aude.

Hedra
A Cornish name that means 'October'.

Heilyn
Originally the word for a cup-bearer in Wales, this is now also used as a girl's name.

Heledd
The earliest Welsh female poet, writing in the seventh century.

Heulwen
Welsh for 'sunshine'.
OTHER FORM: Heulwyn.

Hieretha
The name of a Cornish martyr, which probably means 'virtuous'.

Hilda
The name of a famous abbess of Whitby.

I ~ Girls

Ia
An Irish missionary who founded a church in Cornwall.

Ida
An anglicised version of Íde.

Ide
An influential religious teacher who taught Brendan the voyager.

Igerna
The beautiful wife of a Cornish king. King Uther fell in love with her and married her when her husband was killed.
OTHER FORM: Igraine.

Ilar
The Welsh form of Hilary.

Imogen
It seems that in his play *Cymbeline*, Shakespeare meant to use the name Inogen, which comes from the Gaelic for 'daughter'.

Ina
A Manx name that means 'daughter'.
OTHER FORM: Iney.

Indeg
One of the mistresses of King Arthur.

Indiu
A name borne by an early abbess at Killeavy in Ireland.

Ineda
There was a Cornish saint of this name, which may be connected to the Gaelic for 'flame'.

Inga
A name introduced to Scotland by immigrants from Scandinavia.

Inira
A Welsh name that means 'honour'.

Innes
A Scottish surname that is used as a first name for girls as well as boys.

Inogen

Probably comes from the Gaelic word for 'daughter'.

Iona

The name of the Scottish island where Saint Columba founded his monastery.
OTHER FORMS: Ione, Ionia.

Ionwen

The female version of Ion.

Iorwen

This name means 'beautiful' in Welsh.

Iosbail

A Gaelic version of Isobel.

Irnan

A sorceress who could change shape at will, whose name may be derived from the Gaelic for 'iron'.

Isabella

An Irish princess who married a Norman Earl Marshall of Ireland.

Isbal

A Manx form of Isabel.

Isbeal

A Gaelic version of Isobel.

Iseabail

An Irish or Scottish form of Isobel.
OTHER FORM: Ishbel.

Iseult

The tragic lover of Tristan in the famous romantic story.
OTHER FORMS: Isolda, Isolt, Yseult.

Isla

A Scottish name taken from that of a river in Scotland.

Isot

A name from the Isle of Man, which means 'of Jesus'.

Ita

An Irish saint who founded a religious community in France in the seventh century.

Ivori

A feminine form of Ivor.

Ivory

The Welsh for 'high-born lady' and also a feminine form of Ivor.

J ~ Girls

Jenifer
One of the Cornish forms of Guinevere.

Jenna
The Cornish form of Jane.

Jenniver
One of the Cornish versions of
Guinevere.

Jinn
A Manx name that means 'grace'.

Joannia
A Manx version of Joan.

Jodoc
An early Breton saint bore this name.

Johnet
One of the Manx female forms of John.

Jonee
A Manx female form of John.
OTHER FORM: Joney.

Jony
One of the Manx female forms of John.

Joyce
Possibly from the Breton Saint Jodoc.

Judwara
A martyr, this saint is highly valued as
she is supposed to be good at interceding
on behalf of supplicants.
OTHER FORM: Juthwara.

Juliot
One of the missionary daughters of a
sixth-century king of Powys.

K ~ Girls

Kady
Derived from the Gaelic for 'first'.
OTHER FORM: Kaydi.

Kaitlin
An alternative spelling of Caitlin.

Karel
Found in Brittany as a version of Carola.

Karen
A variation of Cairenn.

Kasey
One of the modern variations of Casey.

Katell
A form of Catherine found in Brittany.

Kathleen
The Irish Gaelic form of Catherine, derived from the word for 'pure'.
OTHER FORMS: Cathleen, Cathline.

Katrina
A version of Catriona.
SHORT FORM: Trina.

Kaytlin
A variation of Caitlin.

Kean
Originally a boy's name that came from the Gaelic Cian, which means 'ancient one', this is now sometimes used for girls.

Keela
This poetic name is taken from a Gaelic word that means 'rare beauty'.
OTHER FORM: Kyla.

Keelin
An anglicised form of Caoilfinn, which means 'slender and fair'.
OTHER FORMS: Kalin, Kaylin.

Keely
Derived from the Gaelic for 'beautiful and graceful'.

Keenan
A first name taken from the surname Kean, which is derived from the Gaelic for 'ancient one'.

Keera

This is an anglicised form of Ciara, which means 'dark' or 'black'.
OTHER FORMS: Keira, Keyra, Kiara, Kiera, Kira, Kyara, Kyra.

Kelly

A transferred surname that mainly comes from Ireland but is also a Manx name.

Kendra

The female form of the Scottish name Kendrick.

Kensa

A Cornish name that means 'first'.

Kentigerna

The name of a famous abbess, named after Saint Kentigern, the patron saint of Glasgow.

Kerensa

This Cornish name, which is connected to the Welsh for 'love', is starting to become popular.

Keria

One of the missionary daughters of a sixth-century king of Powys.

Kerra

A Cornish name that means 'dearer'.

Kerry

Taken from the county in Ireland of the same name, this is used for girls as well as boys.
OTHER FORM: Keri.

Kerye

A Cornish saint's name.

Kew

The name of a saint who came from Cornwall.

Keyne

The name of the daughter of a sixth-century king of Powys who was known for her beauty. There was also a Cornish Saint Keyne who was celebrated for her ability to cure illness.
OTHER FORM: Keynwir.

Kiaran

An anglicised form of Ciaran, which can be either male or female, and means 'small dark person'.

Kirree

A pet form of Katherine found on the Isle of Man.

Kirstie

The Scottish form of Christine, which means 'follower of Christ'.
OTHER FORM: Kirsty.

Kody

An alternative spelling of Cody, which means 'good fortune'.

Koulm

This Breton name is derived from Columba, which means 'dove'.

Koulmia

A Breton name meaning 'little dove'.

Krystell

This variation of the name Crystal is to be found in Brittany.

Kyle

The name of a Scottish district. It has links with the Gaelic for 'church' or 'narrow'.

OTHER FORM: Kylie.

Kyna

Could be derived from the Gaelic for 'affection' or for 'champion'.

L ~ Girls

Laban
According to the old sagas she was the wife of Lir, the god of the sea.

Lachtna
Used more often as a boy's name, this is connected to the Gaelic for 'milky complexion'.

Lallóc
The sister of Mel, an early bishop of Ardagh.

Lana
This is a short form of Alana which means 'darling'.

Laorans
A female form of Laurence found in Brittany.

Lasair
An old Irish name that means 'fire' or 'flame' in Gaelic.

Lauon
The sister-in-law of a 13th-century ruler of the Isle of Man.

Laura
From the word for a laurel tree. Traditionally, those excelling in war or artistic endeavour were crowned with a wreath of laurels.
OTHER FORMS: Lora, Loretta, Lori, Lowri.

Lena
A version of Helen found in Brittany.

Lenaig
A Breton form of Helen.

Leri
An affectionate form of Eleri.

Lesley
This Scottish name is probably derived from the Gaelic for 'low-lying meadow'.

Liadan
From the Gaelic that means 'grey lady'. She was a beautiful nun who was loved by the poet Cuirithir but their love was chaste.

Liadin

A seventh-century poet who died of grief when her lover was banished from Ireland.

Liban

In the old myths she lived for 300 years in an Irish lake until a fisherman caught her in a net, after which she became a Christian.

Lileas

A Gaelic version of Lillian.

Lilee

The Manx form of Lily.

Lilidh

A Gaelic version of Lillian.

Lilwen

This Welsh name means 'white lily'.

Linet

A short form of Eiluned.

Lithgen

Meaning 'lucky birth', this is the name of an Irish saint.

Liusaidh

A Gaelic version of Lucy.

Lleucu

A Welsh form of Lucy that can also be translated as 'dear light'.

Llian

The Welsh word for 'flaxen' or 'linen' and therefore appropriate for blonde girls.

Llinos

The Welsh for 'linnet'.

Lluan

A saint and daughter of the Welsh king Brychan.

Lora

The Manx form of Laura.

Lorne

Derived from the Gaelic for 'fox'.
OTHER FORM: Lorn.

Loveday

An old Cornish name that is coming back into fashion.

Lowena

From the Cornish meaning 'joy'.
OTHER FORM: Lowenek.

Lowri

A Welsh form of Laura.

Luisiúil

Derived from the Gaelic for 'glowing'.

Lula

A Manx name that means 'shining'.
OTHER FORM: Lulach.

Luned

One of the heroines in Welsh myths whose name, like Eluned, means 'one who many desire'.
OTHER FORM: Lunet.

Lupait

The name of a nun who was deliberately run over by Saint Patrick's chariot to punish her for living with a monk.

Lynette

This may mean 'little lake' or be a diminutive of Lynda.
OTHER FORM: Lynn.

Lynwen

A Welsh form of Lynn.

M ~ Girls

Mab
This may come from the Welsh for 'child' and is used by Shakespeare as the name of the Fairy Queen in *A Midsummer Night's Dream*.

Maban
Saint Maban was a particularly holy saint who lived in Cornwall.
OTHER FORM: Maben.

Mabin
From the Welsh for 'child' or 'youth'.

Mabyn
One of the missionary daughters of a sixth-century king of Powys.

Macha
A very old name that was borne by an Irish goddess and a historical warrior queen.

Madhbh
A warrior queen in Irish mythology who was very competitive about the size of her herd of cattle and was featured in the tale 'The cattle raid of Cooley'.

Madrun
This Cornish saint's name appears to have been taken in honour of Mary Magdalene.

Maeve
The anglicised version of Medb, who was one of the best known of the mythological heroines.
OTHER FORM: Mave.

Maighsi
One of the Gaelic versions of Margaret.

Mailli
A Cornish form of Mary.
OTHER FORM: Melle.

Mair
A form of Mary that is found in Ireland.

Máire

One of the many Irish versions of Mary or Maria.

OTHER FORMS: Maisre, Mariam, Maure, Miriam.

Mairead

One of the Gaelic forms of Margaret.

Máireen

In the old legends she was the bald wife of a High King.

Mairi

One of the Gaelic forms of Mary.

Mairighead

An Irish form of Margaret.

Maiwen

With the meaning 'beautiful May', this Welsh name is a good choice for a girl born in that month.

Malane

A Manx form of Magdalene.

Malvina

Possibly derived from the Gaelic for 'smooth brow', this name was created in the 18th century by James Macpherson in his *Poems of Ossian*.

Manana

The feminine form of the Manx name Mannanan.

Maolíosa

The Gaelic and Welsh words for 'honey' are thought to be the source of this name.

OTHER FORM: Melissa.

Marcassa

A Breton name, possibly derived from the French word for a wild boar.

Margaid

A Manx name that means 'pearl'.

Marged

A Welsh form of Margaret.

Mari

This variation of Mary is found in Wales as well as in Ireland.

Maria

One of the many variations of Mary.

Mariod

A Manx name meaning 'little Mary'.

OTHER FORM: Mariot.

Marsaili

The Gaelic version of Marjorie.

Mary

An anglicised form of the Irish Máire.
OTHER FORMS: Mailli, Mair, Mairi, Maria, Marya, Mhaeri, Moirrey, Murra.

Maude

The name of a famous Welsh witch, who was conjured up to frighten children.

Maura

A variation of Máire, this is a saint's name.

Maureen

Derived from the Gaelic Móiríne, this means 'little Mary'.
OTHER FORMS: Maurene, Maurine, Moreen.

Mavourna

A poetic name that appears in Irish ballads and has the meaning 'my little darling'.
OTHER FORM: Mavourneen.

Mawde

A diminutive of Matilda or Magdalene, used on the Isle of Man.

May

A diminutive of Mary and also a name in its own right.

Mealla

Three saints bore this name which is probably connected to the word for 'lightning'.

Meara

May be related to the word for 'sea' and could be a transferred surname.

Meave

A Manx name meaning 'fairy queen'.

Medb

From the word 'mead', this literally means 'she who makes men intoxicated' and was the name of a tumultuous warrior queen of Connacht.
OTHER FORMS: Maebh, Méabh, Medbh.

Medwenna

Derived from the Welsh for 'maiden'.

Megan

A Welsh pet form of Margaret that has become a name in its own right.
OTHER FORMS: Maegan, Maygen, Meg, Meghan.

Melangell

He is the patron saint of small animals, and so for centuries in Powys hares were known as 'Melangell's little lambs'.

Melanie

Almost exclusively found in Cornwall until a century or so ago, this was the name of two early saints.

Melissa

An anglicised version of Maolíosa.

Melle

A Breton variation of the Cornish Mailli.

Mellyn

A Cornish name meaning 'yellow-haired'.

Melora

Reputed to be the name of a daughter of King Arthur.

Melyor

A Cornish name, in use up to the 18th century.

Mena

This appears to be the name of a Cornish saint but the facts about her are obscure.

Meredith

Comes from the Welsh surname meaning 'great chief' and is now given to girls as well as boys.
OTHER FORMS: Meredydd, Meredyth, Merideth, Merry.

Merewin

A Cornish saint whose name may derive from the Celtic word for 'maiden'.

Merion

This Welsh name is a variation of Marion.

Merlyn

A female form of the Welsh Merlin.
OTHER FORM: Merlene.

Merteniana

The name of a Cornish missionary in the sixth century.

Mervena

Probably a female version of Marvin or a variation of Merewin.

Meryl

A variation of Muriel, which is best known due to the actress Meryl Streep.
OTHER FORM: Merrill.

Metheven

A Cornish name that means 'June'.

Mhaeri

One of the Gaelic forms of Mary.

Milucrah

A druidess who could perform all sorts of magic.

Miniver

There was a Cornish saint of this name, which is probably a version of Guinevere.

Minver

One of the missionary daughters of a sixth-century king of Powys.

Miriam

One of the many variations of Máire, this is thought to be the name of the mother of Jesus.

OTHER FORM: Mariam.

Mis

In Irish myths she is cured of madness by her lover.

Modwen

A Welsh name that comes from the word for 'maiden'.

Moina

Probably connected to the Gaelic for 'soft and grassy'.

Moira

An anglicised version of the Irish Máire.

OTHER FORMS: Moire, Moyra.

Móiríne

This is a diminutive of Máire and therefore means 'little Mary'.

Moirrey

A Manx version of Mary, this has the meaning 'bitter'.

Mol

The name of a Welsh witch, also known as Maude.

Mona

Derived from a poetic name for the Isle of Man and also the Irish Gaelic for 'good, noble'.

OTHER FORM: Monenna.

Mór

The name of several daughters and wives of kings of Munster in early Irish history.

Morag

A Scottish pet form of Mór, this is no longer confined to Scotland.

More

A Manx name which means 'great'.

Morfydd

Derived from the Welsh for 'maiden' and was the name of a sixth-century princess.
OTHER FORM: Morfudd.

Morgan

Morgan le Fay was the legendary wicked step-sister of King Arthur who is usually thought of as a witch.

Morgane

A form of Morgan found in Brittany.
OTHER FORM: Morganez.

Moriath

A mythical princess reputed to have cured her husband's dumbness.

Morna

Derived from the Irish Gaelic for 'darling', this name is also found in Scotland.

Mórrígán

The goddess of war, death and slaughter in old Irish myths.

Morve

This means 'high peak' in Gaelic and is taken from the name of a district on the west coast of Scotland.

Morveren

A Cornish name meaning 'maid of the sea'.

Morwenna

A Cornish and Welsh name that probably means 'maiden'. There are churches in Cornwall that are dedicated to the fifth-century Saint Morwenna.
SHORT FORM: Mo.

Morwyn

The Welsh word for 'maiden'.

Moya

Originally a variation of Máire but now a name in its own right.
OTHER FORM: Moyenna.

Muadhnait

Derived from the Gaelic for 'noble' or 'good', this is anglicised to Mona.

Mugain

The wife of a High King in early Irish history.

Muire

This Celtic name for the Virgin Mary is usually considered too holy to be given as a first name.

Muiréad

One of the many Irish versions of Margaret.

Muireall

The Gaelic version of Muriel.

Muirgheal

An old Celtic name that means 'bright as the sea'.

Muirne

Taken from the Gaelic for 'beloved'.
OTHER FORMS: Merna, Murna, Myrna.

Mureal

A Manx version of Muriel.

Muriel

An ancient Celtic name meaning 'bright sea'.
OTHER FORMS: Meriel, Merrill, Meryl, Muireall, Mureal.

Murine

Derived from the Gaelic for 'beloved'.

Murphy

This transferred surname has traditionally been a boy's name but is occasionally given to girls.

Murra

A Manx version of Mary.

Mwynen

Derived from the Welsh for 'gentle'.

Myfanwy

This Welsh name means 'my fine little one'.
SHORT FORM: Myfi.

Myrna

From the Irish Gaelic for 'beloved' and a variation of Muirne.
OTHER FORMS: Merna, Murna.

N ~ Girls

Náible
Originally from the French for 'lovable', it was transformed into this Irish Gaelic name.

Nana
Possibly connected to the Gaelic for 'nine' but also a variation of Nanna.

Nancy
Possibly a variation of Agnes.
SHORT FORM: Nan.

Nanna
Although associated with grandmothers, this was the name of a very early goddess of flowers.
OTHER FORM: Nana.

Nant
A Welsh name that means 'stream'.

Nápla
An Irish version of a Norman name derived from the French for 'lovable'.

Nárbflhfhlaith
This means 'noble princess'. An early bearer of this name was married to the abbot of Trim.

Navlin
A blend of two Gaelic words, this means 'sacred pool'.
OTHER FORM: Newlyn.

Neala
This Irish name is a female form of Niall.
OTHER FORM: Neila.

Neillidh
A Gaelic version of Helen.

Nelda
A female form of Neil.
OTHER FORM: Nilda.

Nemetona
A Celtic goddess, guardian of the sacred oak groves where the druids performed their rites.

Nerys

The female form of the Welsh for 'lord' so could be said to mean 'lady'.

Ness

A mythical ambitious female from Ulster.

Nessa

This may come from the Gaelic for 'secret' or more probably means 'not gentle'. It was the name of the mother of Conchobhar.

OTHER FORMS: Neasa, Nessie.

Nest

In the early 12th century she appeared in the Welsh chronicles as 'the most beautiful woman in the country'.

Nesta

A Welsh pet form of Agnes.

Nevidd

Derived from a word that means 'holy place', this Celtic name was used in Cornwall as well as Wales.

OTHER FORM: Nevydd.

Newlyn

A variation of Navlin but also the name of a seaside town in Cornwall.

Niamh

In Irish Gaelic this means 'radiance'. She was a goddess who fell in love with the son of Finn Mac Cool and took him to the land of perpetual youth.

OTHER FORM: Néamh.

Nodhlaig

Derived from the Irish for Christmas, this is the equivalent of the French Noelle.

OTHER FORMS: Nollaig, Nollaigín.

Nolwenn

A Breton saint whose festival is in July.

Nonita

A Cornish variation of Nonn.

Nonn

From Brittany and Cornwall, this may mean 'nun' or be associated with a ninth child.

OTHER FORMS: Nonita, Nonna.

Nora

A short form of the Latin name Honoria, which means 'honour' and is widely used in Ireland.

OTHER FORMS: Noni, Norah, Nore, Noreen.

Nuala

A short form of the Irish Fionnuala,
which means 'white-shouldered'.

OTHER FORM: Nola.

Nuline

This Cornish name is probably a
variation of Newlyn.

O ~ Girls

Oanez
One of the many variations of Agnes, this name is to be found in Brittany.

Odhrán
Although this is the name of a male saint it is also used for girls and means 'dark-haired'.
OTHER FORM: Oran.

Odras
In the myths, she tried to stop a magic bull making off with an old woman's cow, and was turned into a pool of water by the goddess The Mórrígán.

Oighrig
The Gaelic version of Africa.

Olwen
This means 'fair footprint' in Welsh. In the legends her beauty was such that white clover blossomed in her footsteps.
OTHER FORMS: Olwyn, Onwen.

Onnee
A Manx version of Annie.

Onomaris
An early leader of the Celts in their wanderings in southeastern Europe.

Onora
A name that means 'honour'.
OTHER FORM: Onnor.

Oonagh
A variation of the Gaelic name Una.
OTHER FORM: Oona.

Orchil
A goddess of the dusk, her name comes either from the Gaelic for 'dark-haired' or the word for 'prayer'.

Orin
Probably derived from the Gaelic for 'gold' and thus means 'golden-haired'.

Orla
This Irish name comes from the Gaelic for 'golden princess'.

Orlaith

The sister of Brian Boru in 12th-century Ireland.

OTHER FORM: Orfhlaith.

Orna

Derived from the Gaelic for 'grey-brown' or 'dark', this was the name of several early saints. It is also the female form of Odhar, which means 'otter'.

Oronwen

A variation of Bronwen.

Oweena

A name that means 'well-born' in Welsh.

P ~ Girls

Paaie
The Manx form of Peggy.

Padraigín
The female form of Padraig.
OTHER FORM: Paidrigin.

Paili
The Irish version of Polly.

Patricia
The female form of Patrick.
OTHER FORMS: Paddy, Paití, Pat, Patsy.

Peggy
Usually thought of as a diminutive of Margaret, this is a very popular name in Scotland, Ireland and the Isle of Man.
OTHER FORMS: Paaie, Pegeen, Peig, Peigí, Peigin.

Penardun
In Celtic myths she was the wife of Llyr, the sea god.

Peri
Welsh for 'pearl'.

Petronilla
An Irish maid to the famous Dame Alice Outlawe, she was burnt for heresy in the 14th century.

Piala
The name of a Celtic Christian missionary who was martyred in Cornwall.

Proinséas
The Irish equivalent of Frances.
OTHER FORM: Pronsaisin.

Q ~ Girls

Quillane
A transferred surname that might be derived from the Gaelic for 'fair maiden'.

Quinnie
Either the female form of Quinn or a variation of the Breton name Kinnie.

R ~ Girls

Radha
This is linked with two different Gaelic words meaning 'vision' and 'red'.

Rae
Derived from the Gaelic for 'moon'.

Raghnaid
The Scottish feminine form of Randal, which means 'great power'.

Raghnailt
The Irish and Manx feminine form of Randal, which means 'great power'.

Raichbhe
A name from early Celtic times borne by the sister of the Irish Saint Kieron.

Ranhilda
A Manx name meaning 'God's fight'.

Raonaid
The Gaelic version of Rachel.

Rathnait
An Irish saint's name that comes from the Gaelic for 'grace' and 'good fortune'.

Reanna
An anglicised version of Rhianna.

Regan
Shakespeare used this name, which means 'king's child', for one of King Lear's daughters.

Reina
This means 'queen' and is to be found on the Isle of Man.

Renny
A Manx name meaning 'fern'.

Reynilt
A Manx name dating from the 12th century.
OTHER FORM: Ragnild.

Rhedyn
Welsh for 'fern'.

Rhiannon

In Welsh myths she was the beautiful daughter of the king of the Underworld. Her name means 'moon goddess'.
OTHER FORMS: Rhian, Rhianna, Riannon, Rigantona.

Rhianwen

Welsh for 'pure maiden'.

Rhona

From the name of an island in Scotland.

Rhonda

Derived from the Gaelic for 'powerful river', this is the name of a Welsh region.

Rhonwen

A Welsh name that means 'white lance'.

Ríbh

An Irish name that has links with the word for 'striped'. The story has it that you will have good luck if you can stroke Ríbh's striped cat.

Richeal

The name of an Irish saint.

Rígnach

An instructor at the religious community at Clonard in the early Celtic Church.

Ríona

An Irish name that means 'queen-like'. There are known to have been two saints with this name.
OTHER FORM: Ríonach.

Riwanon

The Breton version of Rhiannon, which means 'moon goddess' or 'nymph'.

Roda

A feminine form of Roden.

Róisín

Meaning 'little rose', this romantic name has been in use in Ireland for several centuries.
OTHER FORM: Rosaleen.

Rona

Possibly derived from the Gaelic for 'seal'.

Rónait

The mother of the abbot of Iona, it is said that she requested that he should pass a 'law of the innocents' to protect non-combatants in war.

Rori

A feminine form of Rory.
OTHER FORM: Ruarí.

Ros
A Scottish form of Rose.

Rosaleen
An anglicised version of Róisín.

Roseen
A Manx name meaning 'little rose'.

Rosen
A Cornish form of Rose.

Rosmerta
An ancient Celtic goddess whose name is related to the Gaelic for 'seed'.

Rowena
This may derive from the Gaelic for 'fair' or 'little redhead'.

Rozenn
A name meaning 'rose' that comes from Brittany.

Ryanne
A feminine version of Ryan, derived from the Gaelic for 'king'.

S ~ Girls

Sabrann
The name of an ancient goddess.

Sadhbh
This name, meaning 'sweet', was that of the wife of Finn Mac Cool who was magically changed into a deer. She was the mother of Oisín, which means 'little deer'.

Saoirse
An Irish name that means 'freedom', which has only been in use since the 20th century.

Saorla
This old name means 'noble princess'.

Sara
With the emphasis placed equally on both syllables, this is the Gaelic version of Sarah.

Saraid
Traditionally reputed to be the forebear of the Gaelic-speaking inhabitants of Scotland, her name means 'best' or 'excellent'.

Scáthach
One of the greatest Scottish female warriors whom Cúchulainn chose to teach him the art of weaponry. The name means 'shadowy one'.

Sceanbh
The wife of a magical harpist in the Irish sagas.

Scenmed
A fierce female warrior in the Irish sagas.

Scoithniamh
A name that means 'lustrous blossom'.

Scoth
This means 'bloom' or 'blossom'.

Sean

Although this is the Irish form of John, the name is also used for girls.

Séarlait

The Irish equivalent of Charlotte.

Seasaidh

A Gaelic version of Jessie.

Seirial

This Welsh name comes from the word for 'brightness'.

Seirian

A Welsh name probably derived from the word for 'sparkling'.

Selma

Saint Selma fought against slavery and the name means 'fair' or 'beautiful'.

Senara

The name of a Cornish saint.

Senga

A Gaelic version of Agnes.

Seona

The Gaelic equivalent of Shona.

Seonaid

A Scottish Gaelic version of Janet.

Seorsag

A Gaelic version of Georgina.

Seosaimhín

The Irish version of Josephine.

Sererena

A Cornish saint who was martyred along with thousands of other virgins.

Seva

A Breton name that means 'peace' or 'tranquillity'.
OTHER FORM: Seve.

Shanley

Taken from the Gaelic words for 'old' and 'warrior'.

Shannon

Derived from the Shannon, the longest river in Ireland, this name means 'old one'.
OTHER FORMS: Shanna, Shannagh, Shannan, Shannen.

Sheela

A variation of Cecilia found on the Isle of Man.

Sheena

The anglicised form of Sine.

Sheila
The anglicised form of Sile.

Shibley
A Celtic form of Isabel which itself is a version of Elisabeth.

Shona
The female form of the Irish name Sean.
OTHER FORMS: Seona, Shuna.

Sian
The Welsh form of Jane, this is well known due to the actress Sian Phillips.

Sibéal
A Celtic form of Isabel.

Sidan
From the Welsh word for 'silk'.

Sile
The Irish form of Cecilia.
OTHER FORM: Sheila.

Sileas
A Gaelic version of Julie.

Simeog
A Gaelic version of Jemima.

Sín
The old Irish word for 'storm', this was the name of a beautiful druidess in the sagas.

Sine
The Irish form of Jane.
OTHER FORM: Sheena.

Sinead
Well known due to the actress Sinead Cusack, this is the Irish form of Janet.
OTHER FORM: Shaynee.

Siobhan
This comes from the Gaelic for 'lily' or for 'God is gracious'.
OTHER FORMS: Chevonne, Shevaun, Síubhan, Siún.

Síomha
An old name derived from the Gaelic word for 'peace'.

Sitofolla
One of the few British Celtic saints whose life was chronicled before AD 1000. She did missionary work among her fellow Celts.
OTHER FORM: Sativola.

Siusaidh
A Gaelic version of Susan.

Sive

An Irish name that comes from the Gaelic for 'sweet'.

Skye

Taken from the name of the island off the coast of Scotland.

Slaney

An Irish surname derived from the Gaelic for 'challenge'.

Soaz

A Breton version of Frances.

Sochla

An old name that belonged to the mothers of two early saints and which means 'of good repute'.

Sorcha

This traditional name means 'brightness' or 'radiance' in Gaelic.

Sowena

A Cornish name meaning 'success'.

Steren

A Cornish name that means 'star'.

Sulwyn

Taken from the Welsh for 'fair as the sun'.

T ~ Girls

Tailtu
The daughter of an early Irish king.

Tamsyn
A Cornish name that is the equivalent of Thomasina.
OTHER FORMS: Tamasin, Tamsin, Tamzin.

Tangwystl
A missionary daughter of Brychan, a sixth-century king of Powys, this name is derived from the Welsh for 'peace'.

Tara
From an ancient fortress, dating back to at least 2000 BC, where the legendary Irish High Kings were consecrated.

Teamhair
The wife of the first Milesian king, Eremon.
OTHER FORM: Tea.

Teasaidh
A Gaelic version of Jessie.

Teath
She was one of the children of Brychan, a sixth-century king of Powys.

Tecca
A Cornish name that means 'fairer'.

Tegan
In Cornwall this name means 'pretty thing' and in Wales it means 'beautiful'.

Tegwen
From the Welsh for 'beautiful and pure'.
OTHER FORM: Tegwyn.

Teneu
An early Christian princess in Scotland.

Tierney
A transferred surname that means 'lordly' in Gaelic.
OTHER FORMS: Tearney, Teerney.

Tirion
This means 'gentle' in Welsh.

Tissot

A Manx name that means 'a gleaner'.

Tlachtga

A goddess, she was the daughter of a solar deity.

Tosha

A Manx name that means 'the first'.

Treasa

An Irish form of Teresa, which means 'strength'.
OTHER FORM: Trea.

Tregereth

This Cornish name means 'compassion' or 'mercy'.

Trina

A short form of Catrina.

Triona

A short form of Catriona.

Tryfena

The Cornish form of Tryphina.

Tryphina

The heroine of a Breton story who was married to Mark, the ruler of Cornwall and Brittany.
OTHER FORM: Tryfena.

Tuathla

An eighth-century queen of Leinster whose name means 'princess of the people'.

Tudful

The name of an early Welsh martyr who was the daughter of Brychan.

Tullia

In Gaelic this means 'peaceful one'.

Tyrona

Taken from the name of County Tyrone in Ireland.
OTHER FORM: Tyronee.

U ~ Girls

Uallach
With the meaning 'arrogant', this was the name of the chief poetess in 10th-century Ireland.
OTHER FORM: Ulluach.

Uathach
The daughter of a mythical female warrior, her name means 'spectre'.

Uilleag
The Gaelic version of Wilma.

Ula
A name that means 'altar' or 'tomb'.
OTHER FORM: Yula.

Ultána
The feminine form of Ultán, which denotes someone who comes from Ulster.

Una
A name that was known in 14th-century Ireland. She was the mother of the legendary Conn of the Hundred Battles.
OTHER FORM: Oonagh.

Ursula
A name meaning 'little wolf' which is found on the Isle of Man.

V ~ Girls

Valma
This Welsh name means 'mayflower'.
OTHER FORM: Valmai.

Vanora
This name means 'white wave'.

Veleda
The name means 'seer' and she was one of the early prophets.

Vevila
This comes from the Gaelic, meaning 'harmonious' or 'melodious'.
OTHER FORMS: Vevan, Vevin.

Vivian
This may be connected to the Norman French meaning 'living'.
OTHER FORMS: Viviane, Vivienne.

Vivien
Derived from the Gaelic for 'fair lady'. She was an enchantress in the tales of the legendary King Arthur.
OTHER FORMS: Viv, Vivanne.

Vorana
A Manx name that means 'great'.

Vorgel
A Manx name meaning 'testimony'.

W, Y ~ Girls

Wallis
More usually a boy's name, this became well known through the American, Wallis Simpson, who married the Duke of Windsor.

Wenhaf
This Welsh name comes from the words for 'fair' and 'summer'.

Wenna
One of the children of Brychan (a sixth-century king of Powys) who became a missionary in Cornwall. Wenna was also a saint.

Winifred
The anglicised name of an early princess, Gwenfrewi, who miraculously came to life after being beheaded and became a nun.
SHORT FORMS: Win, Winnie.

Wovela
A variation of Gulval, the name of a sixth-century Cornish missionary.

Wynne
A Welsh name that comes from the word for 'fair' or 'blessed'.
OTHER FORM: Wyn.

Yanna
A Breton and Cornish name that means 'God is gracious'.

Ygerana
The name of a Duchess of Cornwall, the mother of King Arthur.

Ynyra
A Welsh name that means 'honour'.

Ysbel
A Manx form of Isabel.

Yseult
An alternative spelling of Iseult, the queen who fell in love with Tristan.

Yula
An alternative version of Ula.

A-Z OF
BOYS' NAMES

A ~ Boys

Abban
The name of a Manx saint.

Abloec
The Cornish version of Havelock.
OTHER FORM: Habloc.

Accalon
In the Arthurian legends he was a Breton who plotted to steal King Arthur's sword, Excalibur.

Adaidh
A Gaelic version of Adam.

Adair
A transferred Scottish surname, possibly derived from the Gaelic for 'oak grove'.

Adaue
A Manx version of Adam.

Addis
Derived from the Gaelic for 'flame'.
OTHER FORM: Aidis.

Addison
A transferred Scottish surname.

Adeon
The son of Caradoc, the Welsh ruler.

Adhamh
A Gaelic version of Adam.

Adomnán
A seventh-century abbot of Iona who passed a law to protect non-combatants in war.
OTHER FORM: Adamnan.

Adwen
This Cornish name means 'winged' or 'bright fire'.
OTHER FORM: Adwin.

Aedan
A Manx name meaning 'little fire'.

Aedh
The name of an early ruler of Ireland who drowned in a river in Donegal.
OTHER FORM: Aed.

Ael
The name of an early Breton saint.

Aelhaeran

A Welsh name that means 'iron brow'.
OTHER FORMS: Alhaern, Alhern.

Aengus

The Irish god of love and poetry.

Afagdu

A Welsh name that means 'black river'.

Agron

The masculine form of Agrona, who was a Welsh goddess of war.

Ahearn

From the Gaelic meaning 'owner of horses'.
OTHER FORMS: Aherne, Hearn.

Aidan

The ruler of a Scottish kingdom and ordained by Saint Columba as king of the Scots.
OTHER FORMS: Eadan, Edan.

Aidne

One of the early kings of Connacht.

Ailbhe

The name of an Irish saint in the time of Saint Patrick.
SHORT FORM: Alvy.

Ailean

A Gaelic version of Alan.

Ailig

The Gaelic version of Alec.

Ailill

One of the most popular names in ancient Ireland. He was a king of Connacht and husband of Medb.

Ailpen

The Gaelic form of Alpin, which is mainly used as part of the Scottish surname MacAlpine.

Aindrea

A Gaelic form of Andrew, this means 'manly' or 'courageous'.
OTHER FORM: Aindrias.

Ainiér

A name that first appears in 11th-century Ireland.

Ainlé

A young warrior, the son of a hero of the Red Branch warriors.

Ainsley

A Scottish transferred surname, possibly meaning 'one meadow'.

Alain

The Breton version of Alan.
OTHER FORM: Alein.

Alair

May derive from the Gaelic word for 'salt'.

Alan

Probably a Breton name, meaning 'harmonious'.
OTHER FORMS: Ailean, Alain, Allan, Alun, Ilan.

Aland

A Manx name meaning 'famed ruler'.

Alastair

The Scots Gaelic form of Alexander, 'defender of men'.
OTHER FORMS: Alaisdair, Alaister, Alasdair, Aleister, Alisder, Alister, Alusdur, Sandy.

Alban

Saint Alban was the first British martyr. The name is either derived from a Gaelic word for 'rock' or it could mean 'white'.
OTHER FORM: Albin.

Albanactus

In the legends this was the name of a very early ruler of Scotland.

Albany

A Scottish name derived from the Gaelic for 'rock'.

Albin

The Breton form of Alban.

Albyn

A Manx name possibly derived from the Scottish Colvin.

Aldyn

A Manx name meaning 'wild'.

Alec

A short form of Alexander, of which Alastair is a Scots Gaelic version.
OTHER FORM: Ailig.

Aled

The name of a Welsh river and of a popular modern singer.
OTHER FORM: Aleid.

Alef

A Cornish version of Olaf and the name of an early king of Cornwall.

Aleyn

A Manx name meaning 'famed ruler'.

Alick

A short form of Alexander, of which Alastair is the Scots Gaelic version.

Allowe

This Manx name is probably a variation of the Irish Ailbhe.

Almer

This name was known in medieval times and was either Breton or Cornish.

Alroy

Probably from the Gaelic for 'red-haired'.

Altar

A Manx variation of Walter.

Alun

The Welsh version of Alan.

Amatheon

This Welsh name comes from the word for 'farming'.

Amhlaibh

A Gaelic version of Aulay.

Anarawd

This Welsh name means 'eloquent'.

Andreays

The Manx form of Andrew.

Andrev

The Breton form of Andrew.

Andrew

The patron saint of Scotland and the name of one of Christ's disciples.
OTHER FORMS: Andreays, Andrev, Anndra.

Aneslis

Believed to be the Celtic version of Stanislaus.
OTHER FORM: Ainéislis.

Aneurin

The Welsh form of Honorius, this is one of the oldest names still used in Britain. Aneurin Bevan helped to set up the British National Health Service.
OTHER FORMS: Aneirin, Nye.

Anghus

A Manx variation of Angus.

Angus

From the Gaelic for 'one choice', this is a popular name in Scotland and is also known for a fine breed of cattle.
OTHER FORMS: Anghus, Mingus.

Angwyn

The Welsh for 'very handsome'.

Annan
A transferred Scottish surname that implies someone who lives by a river.

Anndra
A Gaelic form of Andrew.

Aodán
The name of a seventh-century Irish Christian missionary.

Aodh
This was the name of two early Scottish kings and means 'fire'.
OTHER FORM: Aodhgagán.

Aodren
The Breton version of Adrian.

Aonghus
Aonghus Og was the god of love in Irish mythology.

Ardal
The Irish equivalent of Arnold.
OTHER FORM: Ardghal.

Ardan
A young warrior, brother of Ainlé.

Argyle
The name of a place and a clan in Scotland, which means 'place of the Gaels'.

Arlen
An early saint who came from Cornwall.

Armanz
A form of Armand found in Brittany.

Arranz
This name comes from the Cornish word for 'silver'.

Art
The name of an Irish king in the third century.

Artair
A Gaelic form of Arthur.

Arthfael
An old Welsh form of Arthur.

Arthur
The name of the legendary king whose Round Table was the seat of so many knights in shining armour who set out on a quest to try to find the elusive Holy Grail.
OTHER FORMS: Artair, Arthfael, Arthure, Artur, Arzhul.

Arthure
A Manx version of Arthur.

Artur

A variation of Arthur, which probably comes from the word for 'bear'.

Arvel

A Welsh name meaning 'wept over'.

Arzhul

A Breton version of Arthur.

Asketil

A Manx name meaning 'holy vessel'.

Aslac

A Manx name meaning 'lacking of the gods'.

Asmund

A Manx name meaning 'gift of the gods'.

Aspallan

A Manx name meaning 'steps of the gods'.

Athairne

An Ulster poet and druid, he was known as 'the importunate'.

Athol

From a place name in Scotland derived from the Gaelic for 'new Ireland'.

Aulay

The Gaelic equivalent of an old Norse name brought to Scotland from Scandinavia.

OTHER FORMS: Amhlaibh, Awley.

Auliffe

Taken from the name Olaf, which the Vikings brought to Scotland.

OTHER FORM: Awlif.

Auryn

Derived from the Welsh for 'gold'.

Austell

The name of the Cornish godson of Saint Mewan. Saint Austell founded a church in Cornwall.

Austeyn

A Manx name meaning 'venerable'.

Avallach

After being defeated in battle, King Arthur went to King Avallach's kingdom of Avalon to be cured of his life-threatening wounds.

B ~ Boys

Báethchellach
An eighth-century abbot of Trim in county Meath.

Baile
One of a pair of star-crossed lovers in Irish myths.

Baird
A Scottish name meaning 'bard' or 'minstrel'.

Bairn
Derives from the Gaelic for 'child'.

Bairre
A short form of Finbar.

Baithine
The name of the second abbot of Iona at the end of the sixth century.

Baldie
A Scottish form of Archibald.

Balfour
Known mainly as a surname, this is also used in Scotland as a first name.

Balor
An Irish god 'of the evil eye'.

Banadel
The name of an early Welsh king, which probably means 'holy hill'.

Banier
The name of one of King Arthur's Knights of the Round Table.

Banning
Derived from the Gaelic for 'white' or 'fair'.

Banquo
Used by Shakespeare in *Macbeth*, this Scottish name may be derived from the Gaelic for 'white hound'.

Baran
A Manx name meaning 'baron'.

Bard

Bards were Celtic minstrels who had an oral tradition of performing poems and songs. They were honoured at the Welsh Eisteddfods.

Barinthus

The Welsh version of Barnabas.
OTHER FORM: Barnaby.

Barnabas

This biblical name comes from Hebrew but there are many versions used in the Celtic countries.
OTHER FORMS: Barinthus, Barnaib, Barney.

Barnaib

The Irish version of Barnabas.

Barra

Derived from the Gaelic for 'spear' and also found in Ireland as a short form of Finbar.
OTHER FORM: Barris.

Barry

This means 'spear' and was the name of several early Irish Christians.
OTHER FORM: Baz.

Bartholomew

The name of an apostle in the bible, this is the equivalent of the Gaelic Parthalán.
OTHER FORM: Bartley.

Bartley

An Irish version of Bartholomew.

Bastion

This Breton name is a version of Sebastian.

Baudwin

The name of a Breton Knight of the Round Table.

Beacán

The name of a sixth-century Irish saint.

Beagán

An Irish name meaning 'little one'.
OTHER FORM: Beagen.

Bearach

An Irish name meaning 'spear'.
OTHER FORM: Baruch.

Bearnard

The Gaelic form of Bernard.

Beathan

The Scottish form of Benjamin.

Bedivere

One of the Knights of King Arthur's Round Table.
OTHER FORM: Belvedere.

Bedwyr

May be derived from the Welsh for 'boatman'.

Beineón

Derived from the Gaelic for 'mild, kind'.
OTHER FORMS: Benan, Benead, Benignus.

Beltane

From the Gaelic for 'May Day'.

Benesek

A Cornish form of Benedictus.

Benignus

This form of Beineón is found in Brittany.
OTHER FORM: Benniget.

Bernard

A name that means 'brave bear'.
OTHER FORMS: Bearnard, Bernez.

Bernez

A Breton form of Bernard.

Bertram

This Manx name means 'bright raven'.
OTHER FORM: Bertrem.

Berwin

The name of an early Cornish or Welsh saint.
OTHER FORMS: Breward, Brewin.

Beuno

An early Welsh saint who was reputed to have miraculously put the head back onto a beheaded woman and saved her life.

Beuzec

A Breton saint who was born to a woman while she was cast adrift at sea. Later they were washed ashore in Ireland.

Bevan

A common surname in Wales, this means 'son of a noble man'.
OTHER FORM: Bevin.

Bhaltair

The Gaelic equivalent of Walter.

Bideven

From the Cornish word for 'hawk'.

Biorn

A Manx name meaning 'wolf'.

Bith

One of the first men in the Celtic creation myth.

Bladud

A Celtic king whose name is probably derived from the word for 'wolf'.

Blair

Also used for girls, this Scottish name means 'from the plain'.

Blaise

In the legends he was a magician at the court of King Arthur.
OTHER FORM: Bleiz.

Blar

The Gaelic equivalent of Blair.

Blathmac

The name of an 18th-century monk.

Bleiz

The Breton form of Blaise.

Blyth

This name from Cornwall means 'wolf'.

Bole

A 15th-century Irish archbishop, he wrote to the Pope complaining of the excesses of the Irish aristocracy.

Bors

Sir Bors was a Knight of the Round Table who completed the quest for the Holy Grail.

Bowen

A transferred Welsh surname that means 'son of Owen'.

Bowie

A Welsh name derived from the Gaelic for 'yellow'.

Boyd

A transferred surname that means 'yellow'.

Boyden

May derive from the Gaelic for 'victory'.

Bradan

A Celtic saint whose name means 'salmon'.
OTHER FORMS: Braddan, Braden, Bradie, Brady.

Bran

A mythological ruler of the Island of the Mighty whose name means 'raven'.

Brandubh

A seventh-century Irish king whose name means 'black raven'.

Brannagh

A transferred Welsh surname that comes from the word for 'raven'.

Brannoc

The name of a sixth-century Cornish priest who was reputed to perform many miracles.

OTHER FORM: Brannock.

Branwaladar

The name of a Breton saint or that of the son of the Cornish king Kenon who was also a saint.

Branwell

A Cornish name meaning 'raven's well'.

Brassal

Various legendary Irish kings bore this name.

Brastias

A Cornish Knight of the Round Table at the court of King Arthur.

Breasal

The name of several legendary kings in Ireland.

OTHER FORM: Breasil.

Brecon

The name of a region in Wales, probably derived from the Welsh for 'king'.

Bregon

The founder of the Milesians, who were reputed to be the original Celts in Ireland.

Brendan

Popularly thought to mean 'prince', the best-known bearer of this name was the 'navigator or voyager' who brought Christianity to Ireland. He was reputed to have sailed to America in a boat made of ox hides.

OTHER FORMS: Brandan, Brandin, Brandon, Breandán, Brenáinn.

Brengy

This Cornish name is derived from the words for 'noble' and 'wolf'.

Brennan

Probably derives from the word for 'sorrow' or 'tear'.

SHORT FORM: Bren.

Breoc

This fifth-century Welsh saint was active in both Brittany and Cornwall.

Bres

The husband of the mother goddess Brigid.

Bret

Originally this meant someone from Brittany.

OTHER FORM: Brett.

Bretan

One of the Manx names for a Briton.

OTHER FORM: Bretnach.

Briac

One of the Breton forms of Brian.

OTHER FORM: Briag.

Briagenn

This Breton name means 'strong'.

Brian

The name of one of the sons of the goddess Brigid and also of the famous 11th-century Irish High King, Brian Boru.

OTHER FORMS: Briac, Briant, Brion, Bryan, Bryant.

Brice

There was a fifth-century French saint of this name, which may be derived from the Celtic word for 'alert'.

Bricriú

From the Gaelic for 'freckled' or 'speckled'.

Brig

The name of a famous law-maker.

Bringaid

The name for a property owner of high standing.

Briw

A Manx name meaning 'judge'.

Broc

This means 'badger', an animal venerated by the Celts. The name and its derivatives are still to be found in the original Celtic areas.

OTHER FORM: Brock.

Brocas

An old Scottish name.

Broccan

The name of a seventh-century saint who wrote a hymn to Brigid that still survives.

Brochan

This Breton name may be derived from the word for 'badger'.

Brodie

From the Scots Gaelic for a rampart.

OTHER FORM: Brody.

Bruce

A Scottish transferred surname, most famous for Robert the Bruce who won the Battle of Bannockburn against the English.

Brus

The Gaelic equivalent of Bruce.

Bryce

This Welsh name means 'son of Rhys'.

Brychan

A king of Powys, he was reputed to have between 24 and 34 children, all of whom he gave to the service of the Church and most of whom became saints.

Brydw

One of the sons of the remarkable 'Elen of the Hosts' who worked assiduously for the early Christian Church.

Brymor

From the Welsh for 'hill'.

Bryn

A popular name in Wales and Cornwall, derived from the Welsh for 'hill'.
OTHER FORM: Brin.

Brynach

The Welsh form of Brannoc.

Brynmor

A Welsh place name.

Buadhach

Derived from the Gaelic for 'victorious'.

Buchan

A transferred surname, the name of the barons of Tweedsmuir, of whom the most famous was the writer, John Buchan, who wrote *The 39 Steps*.

Buchanan

A Scottish transferred surname and the name of a clan.

Buddug

The Welsh version of Budog.

Budoc

The patron saint of Cornwall who spent his early years in Ireland. The name may have its roots in the Gaelic for 'victorious'.
OTHER FORM: Budog.

Buthek

This Breton saint was venerated in Cornwall.

C ~ Boys

Cabhán
The name of a place in Ireland, meaning 'grassy hill' or 'hollow', that is sometimes used as a first name.

Cad
A short form of Cadfael or Cedric.

Cadan
An old Cornish name which comes from the word for 'battle'.

Cadell
From the Welsh meaning 'battle spirit'.

Cadeyrn
A Welsh name that means 'battle' and 'strong'.

Cadfael
A Welsh name that is well known due to the character of a medieval monk in a popular television series.
SHORT FORM: Cad.

Cadfan
The Welsh for 'battle peak'.

Cado
A Breton version of Cadoc.

Cadoc
The name of a sixth-century Welsh saint who has many churches dedicated to him.
OTHER FORMS: Caddock, Cado, Cadog.

Cadogan
From the Welsh for 'battle honour'.

Cador
The name of a legendary Cornish king.

Cadwallader
A name meaning 'battle chief', which has been found in Wales since the seventh century.

Cadwallen
Another name that includes the Welsh word for 'battle'.

Caedmon
A member of Saint Hilda's community at Whitby who was known as the earliest 'English' poet.

Cael
From the Gaelic for 'slender'.

Caelan
A Scottish form of Nicholas.

Caerbe
A Manx name meaning 'virtuous love'.

Cahan
The Irish form of Kane.

Cahir
The name of a legendary High King of Ireland.
OTHER FORM: Cahir.

Cai
A variation of Kay, which was the name of King Arthur's steward.

Cailean
A Scottish name taken from the Gaelic for 'the victory of the people'.

Cairbre
A mythological warrior who was the son of a king of Leinster.
OTHER FORM: Cairpre.

Cairn
A Welsh name taken from the pile of stones used as a landmark.

Cairnech
An early Christian bishop, he put a curse on one of the early High Kings for throwing out his wife and daughters for the love of the druidess, Sín.

Calatin
An Irish soldier who was killed in battle by Cúchulainn.

Caley
Derived from the Gaelic for 'slender' and used for girls as well as boys.

Calidore
The name of a brave and gentle Knight of the Round Table.

Calma
A name that means 'valiant'.

Calquhoun
A transferred Scottish surname.
OTHER FORMS: Calhoun, Colquhoun.

Calum
The Gaelic for Columba, which means 'dove'.
OTHER FORM: Callum.

Camber

The legends have it that he was the founder of Wales, that is, Cymru.

Cambeulach

The Gaelic version of Campbell.

Camden

The name of a place and also a surname, this can be used as a first name. It comes from the Gaelic for 'winding valley'.
SHORT FORM: Cam.

Cameron

Meaning 'crooked nose', this is also used as a first name for girls.
OTHER FORM: Camran.

Campbell

Taken from a famous Scottish clan, whose name means either 'crooked mouth' or 'from the battlefield'.
OTHER FORMS: Cambeulach, Campie.

Camran

The Gaelic for Cameron, this means 'crooked nose'.
OTHER FORM: Camryn.

Canank

The name of an early Cornish saint.
OTHER FORM: Canak.

Cane

A Manx name meaning 'one who weeps'.

Canice

A sixth-century Irish missionary who founded churches in Ireland, Scotland and Wales.

Cano

In the old romantic tales he was the Tristan figure who had a love affair with Créd, the Iseult figure.

Caoilte

A swift runner and a member of the Fianna in Ireland.

Caoimhín

Taken from the Gaelic meaning 'handsome' or 'of gentle birth' and has evolved into the name Kevin.
OTHER FORMS: Cavin, Coemgen.

Caolán

The name of two saints, this means 'slender youth'.

Caplait

A druid in seventh-century Ireland who was converted to Christianity by Saint Patrick.

Caractacus

The first-century British chieftain who stood up to the Romans but was captured with his family and taken to Rome where he stayed for the rest of his life.

Caradeg

A Breton name derived from Caractacus.
OTHER FORM: Caradec.

Caradoc

From the Welsh for 'beloved'.
OTHER FORMS: Caradog, Karadoc.

Carannog

A Welsh saint who met Saint Patrick in Ireland and was reputed to have saved King Arthur from being poisoned by a snake.
OTHER FORMS: Carantec, Carantoc, Carantog.

Carbry

A Manx name meaning 'virtuous lord'.

Carey

A transferred surname, which may be derived from the Irish Gaelic for 'dark' or the Welsh for 'castle'.
OTHER FORMS: Cary, Kary.

Carlin

From the Irish Gaelic for 'little champion'.
OTHER FORM: Carling.

Carmac

A Manx name meaning 'charioteer'.
OTHER FORM: Carmick.

Carn

A Welsh name, possibly derived from 'cairn'.

Carne

Originally a Welsh surname. Carne of the Gloucester Regiment fought nobly in the Korean War.

Carney

An Irish name derived from the Gaelic for 'victorious'.

Carollan

This diminutive of Carroll has the meaning 'little champion'.

Caroly

A Manx name meaning 'noble-spirited'.

Carraig

From the Gaelic for 'rock'.

Carrick

From the Irish Gaelic for 'rock'.
OTHER FORM: Carig.

Carroll

May be derived from the Gaelic for 'fierce warrior'.
OTHER FORMS: Carl, Karl.

Carvey

This transferred surname may come from the Gaelic for 'naval'.

Casey

From the Irish Gaelic for 'vigilant in battle'.
OTHER FORM: Caswell.

Cashin

A Manx name meaning 'love'.

Cassidy

An Irish surname, which may come from the word for 'curly-haired'.
SHORT FORM: Cass.

Caswallawn

A mythical Welsh prince whose beloved Fleur was carried away by an enemy, but he never gave up on his search for her.

Cathal

From the Irish Gaelic for 'strong in battle', this was the name of several medieval kings.
OTHER FORM: Cahal.

Cathán

This means 'warrior' in Gaelic.

Cathaoir

Derived from the Gaelic for 'guard'.

Cathmore

An Irish name that means 'great battle'.

Catihern

A sixth-century Breton priest who allowed women to concelebrate Mass with male priests.

Cavan

A place name in Ireland that is sometimes used as a first name.

Ce

The Gaelic version of Keith.

Ceallach

A traditional Irish name that means 'bright-headed'.

Cearbhall

A traditional name that probably means 'fierce and brave warrior'.
OTHER FORM: Cearúil.

Cearnaig

An Irish name that means 'victorious'.
OTHER FORM: Cearney.

Cecil

An old Welsh name that means 'sixth'.

Cedric

This may be of Celtic origin or it may have been made up by Sir Walter Scott in the novel *Ivanhoe*.
OTHER FORMS: Cad, Cerdic.

Cellac

The name of a bishop of Kilmore-Moy.

Celthair

An early Irish warrior, whose name may come from the Gaelic for 'concealment' or 'mask'.

Cernunnos

The name of the ancient Celtic god of fertility.

Cerwyn

This means 'fair love' in Welsh.

Cethern

A hero of old Irish tales.

Cian

A Manx name meaning 'one who weeps'.

Ciarán

This means 'little dark one' and was the name of many Celtic saints.
OTHER FORMS: Ceran, Queran.

Cillian

May come from the Gaelic for 'church'.
OTHER FORMS: Kilian, Killian.

Cimbaeth

A ruler of Ireland in the fourth century BC.

Clancy

This transferred surname is derived from the Gaelic for 'red-haired warrior'.

Clearie

A transferred surname that probably comes from the Gaelic for 'minstrel'.
OTHER FORM: Cleary.

Cledwin

From the Welsh for 'sword'.

Cliamain

The Gaelic version of Clement.

Clunes
A Scottish name from the Gaelic for 'meadow'.

Cluny
One of the Scottish names derived from the Gaelic for 'meadow'.
OTHER FORM: Clooney.

Clydai
The Welsh for 'fame'.

Clyde
Possibly taken from the name of a river in Scotland, it may also mean 'heard from a distance'.
OTHER FORMS: Cly, Clywd.

Clywd
A Welsh form of Clyde.

Coemgen
A Breton form of Caoimhín.

Coinneach
Derived from the Gaelic for 'good-looking'.

Colan
The name of a seventh-century Welsh saint and means 'hazel tree' in Welsh.

Colby
From a place name in the Isle of Man.

Colin
This Irish and Scottish name is derived from the Gaelic for 'puppy' or 'youth'.
OTHER FORMS: Coilin, Col, Cole, Collen.

Coll
An old Irish name that means 'high chief'.

Colla
A Manx name meaning 'highest'.

Colm
One of many names derived from the Latin word for a dove.
OTHER FORM: Coulm.

Colmán
This is a version of Columbanus and also of Columba, and there have been many holy people, musicians and poets with this name.

Colmcille
The name means 'dove of the church'. Saint Columba, a monk in sixth-century Ireland who founded the famous monastery in Iona in Scotland, was also known by this name.

Colum

A short version of Columba or of Malcolm.

Columba

An Irish saint who founded a famous monastery at Iona in the Scottish islands, which became the centre of Christianity in Scotland.
SHORT FORM: Colum.

Colwyn

The name of a place in Wales, this means 'hazel grower'.

Colyn

A Manx name meaning 'whelp'.

Combghall

A follower of Saint Columba who founded a monastery at Bangor.

Con

A short form of Conan or Conal.

Conaire

The name of an Irish warrior.

Conal

A Manx name that means 'love'.
SHORT FORM: Con.

Conall

An Irish champion warrior who appears in old heroic tales.

Conan

The name of one of the great Irish kings, and also of a legendary Cornish king, this means 'hound' or 'wolf'.
OTHER FORMS: Con, Kenan, Konan, Kynon.

Conchobar

A name meaning 'lover of hounds'. He was also a king in the old Irish myths.
OTHER FORM: Conchur.

Condal

In Irish mythology, he was the son of Conn.
OTHER FORM: Condle.

Conganchas

A magic spell made him indestructible: he could not be wounded except through the sole of his foot, but his secret was discovered by his wife Niamh who had only married him in order to find it out.

Conlaed

A bishop who helped Saint Brigid run her religious community in the sixth century and who was possibly her husband.

Conlan

This Irish name may be derived from the Gaelic for 'endeavour'.

OTHER FORMS: Conlin, Conlon.

Conlaoch

From the Gaelic for 'noble lord'.

OTHER FORMS: Conla, Conleth.

Conn

From the Gaelic word for 'noble one', this was the name of a famous historical Irish king, Conn of the Hundred Battles.

Connaghyn

The name of a Manx saint to whom Kirk Conchan was dedicated.

Connell

Popular both as a first name and as a surname, this comes from the Gaelic for 'strong as a wolf hound'.

Connor

An old Irish name that is an anglicised version of the Gaelic name Conchobar.

OTHER FORM: Conny.

Conway

Although this is the name of a place in Wales, it is also found as a first name in Ireland, the Isle of Man and Scotland.

OTHER FORM: Conwy.

Conylt

A Manx name meaning 'love'.

Coobragh

The Manx form of Cuthbert.

Cooil

A Manx name meaning 'courageous'.

Corc

An old Irish name borne by the king of Munster, which means 'red'.

OTHER FORM: Corcán.

Corcrán

From the Gaelic for 'crimson'.

OTHER FORMS: Corcoran, Corquoran.

Corentine

A Breton hermit who lived on the flesh of a magical fish. Another, or possibly the same, Cornish-born saint of this name became the first bishop of Quimper in Brittany.

OTHER FORMS: Chorentine, Cury.

Corey

The Irish equivalent of Godfrey.

OTHER FORM: Cory.

Cormac

A Manx name meaning 'charioteer', this is also popular in Ireland and Scotland.
OTHER FORM: Cormick.

Costentyn

Saint Costentyn was a Cornish king who gave up his throne to become a monk.

Craiftín

An Irish harpist of this name played so sweetly that his music could transform whoever heard him into a state of rapture.

Craig

From the Gaelic for 'rock'.

Cranog

From the Welsh word for 'heron'.

Credne

A legendary silversmith who made swords for the gods.
OTHER FORM: Creidne.

Crimthann

This name means 'modest warrior' and he was one of the High Kings of old Ireland.

Críomhtán

This may have been the original name of Saint Columba.

Criostaí

Gaelic for a Christian.
OTHER FORM: Christie.

Crisdean

The Gaelic equivalent of Christopher.

Cristal

The Manx pet form of Christopher.

Cristen

A Manx name meaning 'belonging to Christ'.

Cronán

A number of saints bore this name, which means 'dark-skinned'.
OTHER FORM: Cronin.

Crunnchú

May be derived from the Gaelic for 'prudent'.
OTHER FORM: Crionnchú.

Crunniuc

The name of an early king of Ulster.

Cualann

An enlightened Irishman who sent his daughter to be educated alongside the boys.

Cubi

In the third or fourth century, this Cornishman converted to Christianity and became the bishop of Poitiers in France.
OTHER FORM: Cybi.

Cúchulainn

The name of a famous warrior, whose heroic deeds were chronicled in ancient Irish tales.

Cuilliok

From the Cornish word for 'soothsayer'.

Cuimmíne

An author of influential work on canon law in seventh-century Ireland.

Cuirithir

A seventh-century Irish poet who was in love with a female poet who became a nun. When he left Ireland for good she lay down and died of grief.

Cuithbeirt

A Gaelic version of Cuthbert.

Cullan

From the Gaelic for 'young'.
OTHER FORM: Cullen.

Culwych

The name of King Arthur's nephew, who won his beloved Olwen by performing Herculean feats of magic.

Cumal

This name has two very different meanings: 'slave' or 'champion'.

Cunotigern

A variation of Kentigern, which means 'hound lord'.

Cury

The Cornish version of Corentine.

Custal

A Manx name meaning 'belonging to Christ'.

Cuthbert

Saint Cuthbert was a bishop of Lindisfarne in the seventh century, whose name means 'well known'.
OTHER FORMS: Cathbad, Coobragh, Cuithbeirt.

Cynan

A brother of Elen Luyddog, who was a leader of the British colonisation of Brittany in the fifth century.

Cynddylan

A British Celtic chieftain who was killed in battle by Oswiu of Northumbria.

Cynfael

From the Welsh for 'chief' and 'prince'.

Cynfor

The Welsh for 'great chief'.

Cyngen

From the Welsh for 'chief's son'.

Cynog

A sixth-century Welsh saint who is associated with many churches in Wales.

Cynon

A son of Cynddylan, he was a strong warrior.

Cynwrig

The name of a 13th-century Welsh prince which means 'royal ruler'.

Cynyr

The name of the grandfather of Saint David who lived in the sixth century.

Cystennin

One of the sons of Elen Luyddog, whose tomb is in Gwynedd.

D ~ Boys

Dacey
From the Gaelic for 'southern'.

Dafydd
The Welsh form of David, this was the name of some early poets.

Dagda
Father of the gods and a god of poetry, arts and crafts.

Dagonet
The name of a jester at the court of King Arthur.

Dai
One of several forms of David to be found in Wales.

Daibhidh
The Gaelic version of David.

Dáire
Taken from the name of a god, this means 'fruitful' in Gaelic.
OTHER FORM: Darry.

Dáithí
A war-like king of this name, which means 'swiftness', lived in fifth-century Ireland.
OTHER FORMS: Dahy, Dathy.

Dálach
An Irish name connected to the word for 'meeting'.
OTHER FORM: Dálaigh.

Daley
From the Gaelic word for 'parliament' or 'assembly'.
OTHER FORM: Daly.

Dalziel
From the Scots Gaelic for 'from the little field'.
OTHER FORM: Dalzell.

Dara
Also used as a girl's name, this comes from the Gaelic for 'from the oak'.
OTHER FORMS: Darach, Daragh.

Darach
A Scottish form of Dara.

Daragh
An Irish form of Dara.

Darcy
Imported into Ireland after the Norman Conquest, this was originally D'Arcy.
OTHER FORM: Dorsey.

Daren
Probably a diminutive of Dara, meaning 'little oak'.
OTHER FORM: Darran.

Darry
An anglicised version of Dáire.
OTHER FORM: Dary.

Dathy
A variation of Dahy.

Daveth
A pet form of David found in Cornwall.

David
Meaning 'darling' or 'beloved', this name is particularly Welsh and Saint David is the patron saint of Wales.
OTHER FORMS: Dai, Daibhidh, Daveth, Davy, Devi, Divi.

Dawe
A fifth-century Welsh saint reputed to have founded a monastery in Cornwall.
OTHER FORM: Docwina.

Deasmhumhain
The old form of Desmond, meaning 'man from Deas Mumhan'.

Deasun
Originally someone of this name would have been an inhabitant of Desmond in south Munster.

Declan
One of the early Irish Christians who may have preached in Ireland before Saint Patrick.
OTHER FORM: Deaglan.

Deiniol
An ancient Welsh name of Celtic origin.

Delaney
A transferred Irish surname connected to the Gaelic for 'challenger'.

Demetus
The founder of the dynasty that ruled Dyfed in the fifth century.

Demne

This Irish name of unknown origin was the original name of Fionn Mac Cool.
OTHER FORM: Deimhne.

Deniel

This Breton name is a version of Daniel, which was originally a biblical name.

Denzel

This transferred surname comes from Cornwall and may originally have evolved from Dionysus.
OTHER FORM: Denzil.

Derry

Although this can be a short form of Dermot or Derek, it may also be derived from the Gaelic for 'oak-like'.

Derwent

The name of several rivers in Britain and means 'clear water'.

Desmond

From the Irish surname meaning 'man from Munster'.
OTHER FORMS: Deasmhumhain, Des, Desi, Dezi.

Devi

A Breton short form of David.

Devin

From the Celtic for 'poet' or possibly 'gift'.
OTHER FORMS: Devan, Devon.

Devlin

From the surname which started as a nickname and means 'brave and strong'.

Dewi

Dewi Sant was popularly known as Saint David, and he is the patron saint of Wales.

Dhone

A Manx name meaning 'brown warrior'.

Diancecht

The Irish god of medicine and an accomplished doctor who made a silver hand for King Nuada who had lost his right arm in battle.
SHORT FORM: Dian.

Diarmad

Probably meaning 'without envy', variations of this name have been held by many illustrious Irishmen through the centuries.

Diarmait

A version of Dermot. Diarmate Mac Murchade is blamed for 'inviting' the Anglo-Normans to invade Ireland and thus starting the troubled relationship between England and Ireland.
OTHER FORM: Diarmaid.

Diarmuid

One of the Irish myths tells the story of Diarmuid, who eloped with Gráinne, a High King's daughter, on the eve on her marriage.

OTHER FORMS: Darby, Derby, Dermot, Diarmid.

Digory

A popular Cornish name until the 20th century.

Dillon

Probably means 'faithful' or 'loyal'.

Dinan

The name of a town in Brittany, occasionally used as a first name.

Dinertach

A 10th-century tragic poem tells of the death of a warrior of this name.

Dion

A Welsh name that has been borne by many saints.

Dionnsaí

An Irish form of Denis.

Dithorba

A ruler of Ireland in the fourth century.

Diuran

In the old legends he was cured of bad scars on his body by diving into a magical lake.

Divi

A Breton short form of David.

Diwrnach

The name of a Welsh giant whose magical cooking pot would only cook the food of brave men, not that of cowards.

Docco

A Cornish saint to whom the church of Saint Kew was dedicated.

OTHER FORM: Dochau.

Doddy

A Scottish short form of George.

Dofnald

A Manx version of Donald.

Dogan

A Manx name meaning 'little dark man'.

Dogmael

This Breton saint has churches dedicated to him in Cornwall as well as Brittany.

Dolan

This transferred surname may come from the Gaelic for 'black'.

Dollin

A Manx name meaning 'world ruler'.
OTHER FORMS: Dolen, Dolyn.

Domhnall

A High King of Ireland in the seventh century.

Domnall

A 17th-century Irish priest.

Domnuil

A king of Alba (Scotland) in the ninth century.

Donach

An Irish variation of Donachan.
OTHER FORM: Donagh.

Donachan

A Manx name meaning 'brown warrior'.
OTHER FORMS: Donach, Doncan.

Donal

An Irish name derived from the Gaelic for 'world' and 'rule'.

Donald

One of the most popular names in Scotland, this means 'ruler of the world'.
OTHER FORM: Dofnald.

Donasien

A Celtic form of Dionysus.

Donn

A god of the dead who guarded the entrance to the underworld.

Donnan

An Irish saint who founded a monastic community on the island of Eigg.

Donnchad

This means 'brown-haired warrior'. In the Irish myths a knight of this name battled with death until death was forced to give up his hold and allow Donnchad to live.

Donnel

From the Gaelic for 'hill fort'.
OTHER FORM: Donnelly.

Donnelly

More often a surname, this is a variation of Donnel.

Donough

Another name from the Gaelic for 'brown-haired warrior'.

Donovan

A very old Irish name which may be derived from the Gaelic for 'little dark one'.

Donyerth

An old Cornish name that probably means 'black ridge'.

Dooil

A Manx name meaning 'dark stranger'.

Doolish

A Manx version of Douglas.

Dorian

A name that may come from the word for 'exile', it was used by Oscar Wilde in *The Picture of Dorian Gray*.

OTHER FORM: Doran.

Dorsey

An anglicised version of Darcy.

Dougal

Meaning 'dark stranger', this was a name given by the Irish to the Vikings who came from Denmark.

OTHER FORM: Dugal.

Dougan

Another variation of the Gaelic for 'dark' or 'black'.

OTHER FORMS: Doogan, Dugan.

Douglas

The name of a famous Scots clan, meaning 'black stream'.

OTHER FORMS: Doolish, Doug, Dougie, Duggie, Dughlas.

Doyle

Taken from the Irish surname, this means 'black'.

Drew

This is either an abbreviation of Andrew or it relates to Druid, which means 'wise man'.

Drustan

Probably an older version of Tristan.

Duane

Another variation of the names that come from the word for 'dark'.

OTHER FORM: Dwayne.

Dubhán

This was the name of two saints and means 'dark-skinned' or 'black-haired'.

OTHER FORMS: Duffin.

Dubhlainn

This may mean 'black blade'. In the legends his lover saved him from death by making him a cloak to render him invisible to his enemies.

OTHER FORM: Doolin.

Duff

A Scottish short form of various Gaelic names. Shakespeare used the name Macduff in *Macbeth*.

Duffin

An anglicised form of Dubhán.

Dufgal

A Manx name meaning 'dark stranger'.

Dughlas

The Gaelic version of Douglas.

Duke

A pet form of Marmaduke.

Duncan

The name of two Scottish kings, it means 'dark-skinned warrior'.

SHORT FORM: Dunc.

Dwyfach

In Welsh myths he was one of the people to escape the deluge or flood in the Ark.

Dwyfan

Another of the chosen few who escaped the deluge in the Ark, according to Welsh myths.

Dyfan

The Welsh for 'ruler of the tribe'.

Dylan

The god of the sea and the name of the well-known 20th-century Welsh poet, Dylan Thomas.

Dynawd

This derives from the Welsh for 'given'.

E ~ Boys

Eachan
The Scottish version of Hector, this means 'little horse' in Gaelic.

Eadan
The Gaelic version of Aidan.

Eaghan
A Manx name meaning 'horseman'.

Eamon
The Irish version of Edmond, this means 'prosperity' in Gaelic.
OTHER FORM: Eamonn.

Ean
A Manx name meaning 'well born'.

Easal
The name of a king that may be connected to the Gaelic for 'waterfall'. The story goes that his pigs had magical qualities, and even if they were cooked and eaten they reappeared in their sty exactly as they were before.

Ector
A Manx name meaning 'stout defender'.

Edan
A variation of Aidan.

Edard
A Manx name meaning 'happy keeper'.

Edern
A Breton version of Edward.

Edryd
From the Welsh for 'descent' or 'stock'.

Efflam
In an early Breton story he is a warrior who has to perform three tasks to win the hand of a beautiful princess.

Efnissien
In Irish myths he is a difficult and aggressive man whose name means 'war-like', but his brother Nissien was exactly the opposite and always conciliatory.

Egan

The anglicised form of Aogán, which means 'little fire'.

OTHER FORMS: Egin, Eginer.

Eginer

The Breton equivalent of Egan.

Eglamour

A name from Celtic myths that includes the French word for 'love'. He was a poor but valiant knight who had to kill a dragon to win his loved one.

Eibhear

In the myths he was one of the Milesians who were early inhabitants of Ireland.

OTHER FORM: Eber.

Eiderd

A Scots name derived from the Gaelic for a 'rich guardian'.

Eifion

A Welsh version of Ivan.

Eilir

The Welsh for 'butterfly' or 'spring', this name is also used for girls.

Einion

This means 'anvil' in Welsh.

Eiros

This may come from a Welsh word meaning 'snow'.

Elatha

A handsome prince who fell in love with the goddess Eire, but could not marry her as he was a mortal.

Elcmar

In the old myths this was the name of the husband of the goddess Boan.

Elfed

The Welsh for 'autumn'.

Eliaz

The Breton version of Ellis.

Elidor

In the old legends he was a handsome boy who played with the gods and goddesses until he stole their golden ball. After this he was no longer allowed to go between the mortal and the immortal world.

OTHER FORM: Elidr.

Eliseg

The name of a ninth-century king of Powys.

Ellar

A Scots name derived from the Gaelic for 'steward'.

Elliot

This name from the Scottish Borders is the family name of the Earls of Minto.

OTHER FORM: Eliot.

Ellis

Thought to be derived from the Welsh for 'benevolent'.

OTHER FORMS: Eliaz, Elisud.

Elouan

The Breton version of Elwyn.

Elowen

From the Cornish for 'elm'.

Elphin

A Welsh name that may be derived from the word for 'kind'.

Elvi

Saint Elvi lived in Wales in the fifth century.

Elwyn

This Welsh name is derived from the word for 'fair' or 'kind'.

OTHER FORMS: Elouan, Elwin.

Emilion

The Breton version of Emlyn.

Emlyn

May originally have had links with the biblical name, Emmanuel, which means 'God is with us', or it may come from a place name in Dyfed.

OTHER FORM: Emilion.

Emmet

Taken from the surname of the Irish patriot, Robert Emmet.

Emrys

The Welsh form of Ambrose.

Emwnt

One of the Welsh forms of Edmond.

Emyr

From the Welsh for 'honour'.

Enan

From the Welsh for 'firm'.

Enda

An early Celtic saint who gave up his kingdom to enter the religious life.

Ennis

This is a place name in Ireland but could also be derived from the Gaelic for 'island'.

Eochaid

The name of a mythical High King.

Eoghan

Derived from the Gaelic for 'yew tree', this is the Irish name for County Tyrone.

OTHER FORMS: Ewan, Ewen.

Eoin

One of the Gaelic forms of John.

Eremon

Reputed to have been the name of the first king of the Milesians, who were early settlers in Ireland.

Erin

The old poetic name for Ireland, this means 'peace'.

Erling

A Manx name meaning 'little earl'.

Ernald

A Welsh variation of Arnold.

Ernan

An Irish name derived from the Gaelic for 'iron'.

OTHER FORM: Iarnan.

Erskine

A Scottish transferred surname made famous by Erskine Childers, the Irish politician and author of *Riddle of the Sands*.

Ervin

A variation of Irwin.

Erwan

A Breton form of Irwin.

Erwin

A Welsh form of Irwin.

Esras

A learned magician who owned a magic spear; whoever wielded the spear would be sure to win their battles.

Euan

One of the Scottish variations of John.

Eudard

The Gaelic form of Edward.

Eudav

According to the legend he was the father of Saint Helena, an early convert to Christianity.

Eunan

The more modern Irish equivalent of Adomnán, who was the abbot of Iona in the seventh century.

Eurig

The Welsh for 'gold'.

Euros

Another name from the Welsh for 'gold'.
OTHER FORM: Eurys.

Euroswyd

The second husband of Penardun, the mother of the mythological Irish queen Branwen.

Eurwen

This means 'fair and golden' in Welsh.
OTHER FORM: Eurwyn.

Euryn

This means 'piece of gold' and also 'darling'.

Evan

A Welsh and Breton form of John.

Evin

This is either an Irish name that means 'swift' or a variation of Evan.

Ewing

This Scottish name means 'fiery'.

F ~ Boys

Fachnan
The name of a sixth-century Irish saint, which is also given to girls.

Fagan
A transferred Irish surname, which may be derived from the Gaelic for 'raven'.

Fáilbhe
This old Irish name probably means 'slayer of wolves'.

Falair
Also a girl's name, this is the Gaelic form of Hilary.

Fanch
A Breton form of Francis.

Faolán
This is derived from the word for 'wolf' and was the name of several early saints and kings of Ireland.
OTHER FORM: Felan.

Faolchú
Another name that means 'wolf' or 'wolfhound'.

Faragher
A Manx name meaning 'supreme choice'.

Farquhar
A Scots name derived from the Gaelic for 'dear one'.
OTHER FORMS: Farqar, Fearchar.

Farrell
This transferred surname is an anglicised form of Fergal.
OTHER FORM: Ferrel.

Fayrhare
A Manx name that literally means 'fair-haired'.

Feardomhnach
In the ninth century he compiled the *Book of Armagh,* which included the earlier *Life of Patrick.*

Feardorcha

This Irish name means 'dark man'.

Fearghal

This means 'man of strength' and was the name of an eighth-century king and a saint from the same time.

Fedilimid

The name of a ninth-century king of Munster.

Feichín

There have been five Irish saints with this name, which means either 'battle' or 'raven'.

Feidhlim

An old Irish name derived from the Gaelic for 'constant' or 'faithful'.
OTHER FORM: Felim.

Felimy

An alternative spelling of Phelimy.

Felix

Originally from the Latin for 'happy' this name is used in Brittany, Ireland and Scotland.
OTHER FORM: Filis.

Felys

A Manx name that means 'happy'.

Fenit

A Gaelic name that means 'fawn'.

Feorish

The Manx equivalent of Piers.

Fer

Fer Cherdne was a bard in the Irish sagas who jumped over the cliffs with the faithless wife of a king, thereby killing her as well as himself.

Ferdia

In Irish legends he was a friend of Cúchulainn, but they had to fight a hard duel in which he was finally defeated by the use of magic.
OTHER FORM: Ferdiad.

Fergal

The name of a murderous eighth-century Irish king, which means 'valorous' in Gaelic.
OTHER FORM: Farrell.

Fergie

A diminutive of Fergus, but also used as a name in its own right.

Fergus

Derived from the Gaelic for a 'vigorous man', this was the name of an early king of Ulster.
OTHER FORMS: Fearghas, Feargus.

Ferguson

A transferred surname that comes from Northern Ireland and Scotland.

Ferris

This comes from a surname and is derived from the Gaelic for 'rock'.

Ferrishin

The Manx name for sprites or fairies.

Fiac

A Manx name meaning 'crow'.

Fiachna

The name of King Lir's son, this comes from the Gaelic for 'raven'.
OTHER FORM: Fiach.

Fiachra

An early Irish saint called Fiachra went to live in France and is supposed to have given his name to the horse-drawn cabs in Paris.
OTHER FORMS: Fiacre, Fiakr.

Fianaid

Derived from the Gaelic for 'fawn', this can also be found as a girl's name.
OTHER FORM: Fianait.

Fife

Originally this meant someone who came from Fife in Scotland.
OTHER FORM: Fyfe.

Filip

The Gaelic version of Philip.

Filis

A Breton version of Felix.

Fillan

Saint Fillan was a missionary in Scotland in medieval times. The name comes from the Gaelic for 'wolf'.

Finan

Many saints have borne this name, which may be related to the Gaelic for 'fair' or possibly the word for 'wine'.

Finbar

The name of at least three Irish saints, it comes from the Gaelic for 'fair-haired'.
OTHER FORMS: Bairre, Barra, Fionnbarr, Fymber.

Fineen

In one legend he was a fairy who came from the clouds to cure Cúchulainn's wounds.

Fingal

A legendary Scottish warrior who gave his name to Fingal's Cave.

OTHER FORM: Fionan.

Fíngen

The name of a Munster king.

Fíngín

A chieftain of Munster who, in an old myth, used to visit a female prophet every year and act on her prophecies.

Fingus

A name derived from the Gaelic for 'fair-haired' and 'vigorous'.

Finian

This name comes from the Irish Gaelic and also the Celtic for 'light, fair' and was made popular by James Joyce when he used it for his book *Finian's Rainbow*.

OTHER FORM: Finnian.

Finlay

More widely found as a surname, this comes from the Gaelic for 'fair-haired warrior'.

OTHER FORMS: Findlay, Finley, Finlagh.

Finlo

A Manx name for 'fair Scandinavian'.

Finn

The early legends are full of the magical exploits of the great Irish hero Finn Mac Cool. The name comes from the Gaelic for 'white' or 'fair'.

OTHER FORM: Fionn.

Finnegas

In the Irish sagas he was a poet who guarded the salmon of all knowledge, and when he tasted it while it was being cooked he became filled with knowledge.

Finnen

A teacher in one of the early bardic and ecclesiastical schools in Ireland where young women were taught alongside young men.

Finnian

The name of a sixth-century Celtic saint and also a variation of Finian.

Fintan

The name of a mythical descendant of Noah who was saved from the deluge when it flooded the world.

OTHER FORM: Fiontan.

Fionan

A Gaelic version of Fingal.

Fionn

Originally this was the name of the commander of the Irish king's élite warriors, the Fianna, who were named after him. It is also a variation of Finn.

Fionngal

King of the Isle of Man in the 11th century.

Fítheal

This early Irish name comes from the word for 'goblin' or 'sprite' and was thought to be that of the brother of Finn Mac Cool.

Flaithrí

An Irish name derived from the Gaelic for 'lord'.

Flan

This Manx name means 'ruddy complexioned'.

Flann

An Irish name from the Gaelic for 'blood red'.

Flannagan

This pet form of Flann is also a well-known surname.

Flannan

There was a seventh-century Irish bishop of this name who was also revered in Scotland, and there are islands named after him in the Outer Hebrides.

Flannery

A transferred surname that means 'red eyebrows'.

Flaxney

This is a transferred traditional Manx surname.

Fliathus

This is a name meaning 'royalty'.

Flinn

Derived from the Gaelic for 'bright blood red'.
OTHER FORM: Flynn.

Floyd

A variation of the Welsh name, Lloyd, which means 'grey'.

Fluellen

A variation of Llewellyn.

Flurry

This is connected to the Gaelic word for 'bounteous, copious'.

Fogal

This Manx name means 'under a promise'.

Foillan

The name of an early Irish monk.

Forbaí

The name of the son of Conchobhar Mac Nessa.

Forgal

In the same way as Fergal, this is probably derived from the Gaelic for 'brave'.

Fráech

Probably from the Gaelic for 'heather'.
OTHER FORM: Fraoch.

Franc

This name from the Isle of Man means 'free'.

Frang

A Gaelic version of Francis.

Fransez

A Breton form of Francis.

Fraser

Originally a Norman name, this became a Scottish surname and is now used as a first name.
OTHER FORMS: Frasier, Frazer.

Frassach

The name of an early Irish hermit who was also a saint.
OTHER FORM: Frossach.

Freer

A Manx name meaning 'friar'.

Friseal

The Gaelic equivalent of Fraser.

Frizzell

This is derived from the Gaelic for 'fresh'.

Furbaide

The son of Queen Medb's sister.

Fursa

An early Celtic Christian who helped to convert the Angles to Christianity.

Fynn

A Manx name meaning 'fair'.

G ~ Boys

Gabhan
A Gaelic version of Gavin.

Gadeon
One of the brothers of the fourth-century British empress Elen.

Gael
Probably from the Welsh for 'wild', this is the name for the Gaelic-speaking people of Ireland, Scotland and the Isle of Man.

Gair
A rare Scottish name that may be connected to a nickname for someone who is not tall.

Galahad
Sir Galahad was the son of the legendary Lancelot and the only Knight of the Round Table to reach the Holy Grail.

Galahaut
In the Arthurian legends he was one of Lancelot's close friends.

Galehodin
The brother of Lancelot at King Arthur's court, his name implied that he came from Gaul.

Galen
From the Gaelic for 'little and lively'.

Galfrid
A Manx name meaning 'son of the Briton'.

Gall
Saint Gall accompanied Saint Columba on his mission to Europe in the seventh century.
OTHER FORM: Goll.

Gallagher
A transferred surname partly derived from the Gaelic for 'foreigner'.
OTHER FORM: Galaher.

Galvin
This appears to come from the Gaelic for 'sparrow'.

Gannon

An Irish ruler who gave his name to the town of Dungannon.

Garan

From the Welsh for 'heron'.

Garbhán

An Irish name derived from the word for 'rough'.
OTHER FORMS: Garvan, Garvin.

Gareth

Almost certainly derived from the Welsh for 'civilised, gentle'.
OTHER FORMS: Garry, Garth, Gary, Gerrit, Giraud.

Garod

A Welsh equivalent of Gerald.

Garret

An Irish equivalent of Gareth.

Garth

A version of Gareth, this means 'hill' or 'wood' in Welsh.

Garvey

From the Welsh for 'peace through victory'.
OTHER FORM: Garvie.

Gavan

A Manx name meaning 'smith'.

Gavin

The Scottish version of Gawain.

Gawain

Sir Gawain was one of the legendary Knights of the Round Table. The name comes from the Welsh for 'hawk from the plain'.
OTHER FORMS: Gavin, Gawayne, Gawen.

Gawen

A common name on the Isle of Man until the 19th century, it is also the Cornish form of Gawain.

Geffry

This means 'God's peace' and is a Manx name.

Gellan

The name of an 11th-century Welsh harpist and poet.

Gelvinak

The Cornish name for the curlew bird.

Geraint

A popular name in Wales, known from early Celtic times, connected to the word for 'old man'.
OTHER FORM: Gereint.

Gerallt
A Welsh name made up of old Germanic words for 'spear' and 'rule'.

Gerens
A Cornish king and also the name of a saint.

Gerent
In the Arthurian legends he was married to the beautiful Enid. There are churches dedicated to Saint Gerent in Cornwall and Brittany.

Germain
The name of a saint to whom Kirk German on the Isle of Man is dedicated.

Geróid
The Irish form of Gerald.

Gerrit
A Breton version of Gareth.

Gerwyn
A name that means 'fair love' in Welsh.

Gethin
A Welsh name meaning 'dusky-complexioned'.

Gibbon
A Manx name meaning 'Bridget's servant'.
OTHER FORM: Giubon.

Gilander
A Manx name meaning 'St Andrew's servant'.

Gilaspic
A Manx name meaning 'bishop's servant'.

Gilchrist
Often found as a surname, this means 'servant of Christ' in Gaelic.

Gilcolm
This means 'Columba's servant'.
OTHER FORM: Gilcalm.

Gildas
This name first appears in an old Breton tale and is also found in Wales where a historian with the name was a contemporary of Saint David.
OTHER FORM: Gweltaz.

Gilfaethwy
A name mentioned in early Welsh myths.

Giliasa
A Manx name meaning 'Christ's servant'.

Gilleabart

The name of a 12th-century Irish king, and also of a Scottish saint who founded a religious community for both men and women.

Gillean

This means 'servant of St John' in Gaelic. OTHER FORM: Gilleathain.

Gilleasbaig

The Gaelic for 'servant of a bishop'.

Gillechriosd

A Celtic name that means 'servant of Christ'.

Gilmartin

A Manx name that means 'servant of St Martin'.

Gilmer

The Gaelic for 'servant of the Virgin Mary', this is a Scots name.

Gilmore

A name found on the Isle of Man that means 'Mary's servant'. OTHER FORM: Gilmurra.

Gilno

A name from the Isle of Man that means 'saint's servant'.

Gilrea

A Manx name meaning 'servant of the king'.

Gilroy

One of the names that come from the Gaelic for 'servant' and 'king'.

Giraud

A Breton version of Gareth.

Glastenen

From the Cornish for 'scarlet oak'.

Glen

The Welsh for 'valley'.

Glendon

A combination of the Welsh for 'valley' and 'fortress'.

Glewas

Cornish for 'clear' or 'bright' and is the name of Saint Petroc's nephew, who was also a saint.

Glyn

A Welsh name meaning 'glen' or 'valley'.

Glyndwr

This means 'black valley' in Welsh and was the name of the Welsh hero, whose name is anglicised as Owen Glendower.

Glywys
The name of a sixth-century king of Glamorgan.

Godred
A Manx name meaning 'God's peace'.
SHORT FORM: Gorry.

Goibhniu
The name of the god of smiths.

Golamh
The warrior who, according to myths, set out to conquer Ireland under the name of Míl.

Golvan
From the Cornish word for 'sparrow'.

Gordon
Taken from the name of a Scottish clan, this has been used as a first name since the 19th century.

Gorlas
A Cornish name that means 'very pure'.

Gorman
The name of a king of Munster in Ireland.

Gormley
A variation of Gorman that is more often used as a surname.

Gormond
A Manx name meaning 'spearman'.

Goron
This Cornish name means 'hero'.

Goronwy
A Welsh name of uncertain origin, which was borne by the legendary Lord of Penilyn.

Gorthelyk
This Cornish name means 'very beloved'.

Gowon
One of the names derived from the Gaelic for 'smith'.

Gradlon
A mythical king of Cornouaille in Brittany.

Graham
The name of a Scottish clan, which is often used as a first name.
OTHER FORMS: Graeme, Grahame, Greum.

Graid

This Welsh name means 'heat' or 'ardour'.

Grant

The name of a Scottish clan and also of the 18th president of the United States.

Gregor

There is a Scots clan named MacGregor, but this name is probably derived from the Greek for 'watchful'.
OTHER FORMS: Greg, Grigor, Griogair.

Gregory

Pope Gregory sent Saint Augustine to England and his name was taken up and used by the Celts.
SHORT FORM: Greg.

Greum

A Gaelic version of Graham.

Griffith

Probably derived from the Welsh for 'strong lord'.
OTHER FORMS: Griff, Griffid, Griffin, Gruffud, Gryffyd.

Griogair

A Gaelic version of Gregor.

Gronwy

This name appears way back in the Welsh myths.

Gruyffydd

The brother of the beautiful Nest, he headed a Welsh uprising against the Anglo-Normans in the 12th century.

Guaire

The name of a seventh-century Irish king, it is also recorded as the name of various saints.

Guénole

The name of a sixth-century abbot of the monastery at Landévennec in Brittany.
OTHER FORM: Winwaloe.

Guerar

This Cornish saint is buried in his native Cornwall.

Gurvan

The Breton form of Garvin.

Guthrie

More usually a surname, this comes from the Gaelic for 'war hero'.

Gwair

A knight at the legendary court of King Arthur.

Gwalchmai

This Welsh name is made up of the words for 'falcon' and 'flat land'.

Gwallawg

The name of a sixth-century Welsh king.

Gwallter

The Welsh equivalent of Walter.

Gwaun

A Welsh name derived from the word for 'health'.

Gweltaz

A Breton version of Gildas.

Gwennin

This is found in Brittany and probably means 'fair' or 'white'.

Gwenogfryn

Derived from the Welsh words for 'smiling' and 'hill'.

Gwent

This comes from the name of a Welsh county.

Gwern

In Welsh this means 'alder'.

Gwilherm

The Breton form of William.

Gwill

A Welsh form of Will.

Gwilym

A Welsh form of William.

Gwinear

An early Christian missionary from Ireland who tried to convert the Cornish and was put to death by the local ruler.

Gwion

This means 'elf' in Welsh.

Gwrlais

The name of a mythical ruler in Cornwall.

Gwydion (Gwyddyon)

Possibly a variation of Gideon. In Welsh literature Gwyddyon was named after his mother, Dôn.

Gwyn

In Welsh legends he was the son of Nudd, the sky god.

Gwynedd

Taken from a Welsh place name.

Gwynek

The name of an eighth-century Cornish
saint, which means 'little fair one'.

Gwynfor

A Welsh name meaning 'white' and
'great'.

Gwynllyw

There was a monk of this name in the
early Welsh Church.

H ~ Boys

Habloc
A variation of Abloec.

Haco
The name of a Cornish leader who was bethrothed to a beautiful princess but was tricked out of marrying her at the last minute.
OTHER FORM: Hacon.

Hafgan
The King of the Otherworld, his name comes from the Welsh for 'summer' and 'song'.

Hagen
From the Gaelic for 'little fire'.

Hamish
The Scottish form of the Irish Seamus.

Hamond
This name comes from the Isle of Man and possibly means 'unwed'.

Hane
A Manx name, probably a variation of Thane.

Harold
Originally from Scandinavia, this means 'herald'.

Harvey
Originally a Breton name, this probably means 'worthy in battle'.
OTHER FORM: Herveig.

Hearn
A variation of Ahearn.

Heddwyn
A Welsh version of Edwin.

Hefin
This Welsh name means 'summer, sunny'.

Heilyn
A Welsh name that appears in the old legends, it means 'wine pourer'.

Herman

A Manx name meaning 'warrior'.
OTHER FORM: Heremon.

Hervé

A French name with its origins in
Brittany, it is the equivalent of Harvey.

Hew

A Welsh form of Hugh.

Hewie

A Scottish version of Hugh or Hubert.

Hicca

A nickname for Richard that comes from
Cornwall.

Hogan

May be derived from the Gaelic word for
'youth'.

Howel

The name of the last king of Cornwall.
SHORT FORM: Howe.

Howell

Probably from the Welsh for 'eminent'.
OTHER FORM: Howie.

Huchon

A Manx variation of Hugh.

Hugen

A Manx variation of Hugh.

Hugh

The equivalent of the Irish Aodh.
OTHER FORMS: Hew, Hewett, Hewie,
Huey, Hugo, Huw, Kew, Uisdean.

Huw

A Welsh form of Hugh.

Hywel

A 10th-century Welsh king who was the
first to strike coins for the united Welsh
kingdom.
OTHER FORM: Hywell.

I ~ Boys

Iagen
A Scottish name meaning 'little fiery one'.

Iago
A Welsh form of James.
OTHER FORM: Ianto.

Iain
A Scottish Gaelic form of John.
OTHER FORM: Ian.

Iarnan
A variation of Ernan.

Ibhair
A bishop in fifth-century Ireland.

Idris
A giant in Welsh legends who was an astronomer and magician. His name means 'ardent or impulsive lord'.

Idwal
Derived from the Welsh for 'lord' and 'rampart', this was the name of two 10th-century Welsh kings.

Iefan
A Welsh version of John.

Iestyn
This name means 'just' in Welsh.

Ieuaf
Derived from the Welsh for 'youngest'.

Ieuan
A Welsh version of John.

Ifan
One of the Welsh versions of John.

Ifor
This Welsh name is taken from the word for 'lord'.
OTHER FORMS: Ior, Iver, Ivor.

Ilan
A Welsh form of Alan.

Illiam
A Manx form of William, this was the name of a famous martyr.

Illtud

The name by which Illtyd was known in Brittany, where he was born and where his feast day is still kept.

Illtyd

A fifth-century Welsh saint whose name is derived from the words for 'multitude' and 'land'. He was a famous scholar who founded a college in Wales and introduced the plough to the Welsh.

Inir

From the Welsh for 'honour'.

Innes

The Gaelic for 'island', this is a Scottish clan name.
OTHER FORM: Innis.

Inry

The Manx form of Henry.

Iobhar

From the Gaelic word for 'yew tree'.

Iollan

A brave warrior of this name was part of the household of Conchobhar.
OTHER FORMS: Yollan, Yolland.

Iolo

A Welsh poet who wrote a satire about married clergy in the 14th century.

Iomhar

A Scottish Gaelic form of Evander.

Ionwen

The Welsh for 'fair lord'.

Ior

The original Welsh form of Ifor.

Iorweth

The Welsh for 'worthy lord'.
OTHER FORM: Yorath.

Iorwyn

This Welsh name comes from the words for 'pure' and 'lord'.

Ioseff

The Welsh form of Joseph.

Irfon

Welsh for 'the anointed'.

Irving

Taken from the place name in Scotland, this name is best known due to the songwriter Irving Berlin.
OTHER FORM: Irvine.

Ith

The name of one of the Milesian princes who were early invaders of Ireland.

Ithel

An old Welsh name that probably means 'generous lord'.

Ithnan

Taken from the Welsh for 'strong sailor'.

Iuchar

One of the sons of the goddess Brigid.

Iucharbam

A son of the goddess Brigid.

Ivar

A Manx name meaning 'archer'.
OTHER FORM: Ivanhoe.

Ivi

From the Gaelic for 'yew', this is also the name of a Breton saint.

J ~ Boys

Jacca
The Cornish version of Jack.

Jacut
A Breton form of Jacob.

Jago
A Cornish form of Jacob.
OTHER FORMS: Jagu, Jegu.

Jagu
A Breton variation of Jago.

Jakez
Found in Brittany, this is related to the French Jacques.

Jamys
The Manx form of James, this means 'beguiling'.

Jared
This name is found in Ireland and probably means 'a rose'.
OTHER FORMS: Jareth, Jered.

Jarlath
Saint Jarlath was a sixth-century bishop in Galway who founded a monastery that was renowned for its scholars.

Jegu
A Breton variation of Jago.

Jocelin
This name was common in medieval times and is now found on the Isle of Man.

Jole
A Manx name that is the equivalent of Yule.

Jonty
An anglicised form of the Gaelic for 'little John'.

Jory
The Cornish nickname for George.

Jos
A Breton form of Joseph.

Jowan

The Cornish for 'God is gracious'.

Juan

A variation of John to be found on the
Isle of Man.

K ~ Boys

Kadec
A variation of Cadoc, this name is found in Brittany.

Kadeg
A Breton variation of Cadog.

Kane
Derived from the Gaelic for 'tribute', this is an Irish name.
OTHER FORM: Cahan.

Karadoc
To be found in Brittany, this is a variation of Caradoc.

Karanteg
One of the Breton forms of Carantog.

Karl
A version of Carroll, which comes from an old Celtic name that probably meant 'fierce warrior'.

Kary
Another way of spelling Carey, which is connected to the Welsh for 'beloved'.

Kay
Sir Kay was one of the knights at King Arthur's Round Table and the king's right-hand man.
OTHER FORMS: Cai, Ka, Kai, Kea, Key.

Kea
The name of a sixth-century Cornish saint and an alternative spelling of Kay.

Kean
A transferred Irish surname, which might have been derived from the Gaelic for 'ancient'.

Keegan
An anglicised form of a Gaelic surname.

Keir
Taken from the Scottish surname, this is best known from the Labour politician Keir Hardy.

Keird
A Manx name meaning 'smith'.

Keith

Probably derived from the Gaelic for 'woods', this was originally a Scottish surname.

OTHER FORM: Cè.

Kelly

A surname found widely in Ireland and also the Isle of Man, it is now used as a first name for girls as well as boys.

Kelvin

The name of a Scottish river that runs through Glasgow, this is used both as a surname and a first name.

Kenan

A Cornish form of Conan.

Kendrick

Found mainly in Scotland, this may come from the Gaelic for 'son of Henry'.

OTHER FORM: Kenrick.

Kennagh

From the Gaelic for 'born of fire'.

Kennedy

An Irish and Scottish surname that is used as a first name, it became popular due to the American President John F. Kennedy.

Kenneth

There was a sixth-century Irish saint of this name who also spent time in Scotland and Wales.

Kent

This comes from an old Celtic word that means 'border'. It is also used as a short form of Kentigern.

Kentigern

The bishop of Strathclyde and Cumbria, he founded a monastic community in Glasgow.

SHORT FORM: Kent.

Kenver

An old Cornish name meaning 'great chief'.

Kenwyn

An old Cornish name meaning 'splendid chief'.

Kermode

A more acceptable version of the Irish name Kermit, both of which come from the name MacDermot.

Kerr

Possibly derived from the Gaelic for 'spear', this Scottish name is a transferred surname.

Kerron
A Manx name meaning 'grey' or 'dark'.

Kerry
Taken from a county in Ireland and more frequently a girl's name.

Kester
A Scottish form of Christopher.

Kevern
The name of a sixth-century Cornish saint.

Kevin
A sixth-century saint, one of the patron saints of Dublin. The name means 'handsome child' in Gaelic.
OTHER FORMS: Kev, Kevan, Keven.

Kew
The Cornish form of Hugh.

Key
Possibly a first name taken from the surname McKee or it can be a variation of Kay.

Kieran
The name of a fifth-century Irish saint whose festival is still kept in Brittany.

Kilian
The Breton form of Killian.

Killian
The name of various Irish saints, this is the anglicised form of the Gaelic Cillian.

Kitto
A Cornish pet form of Christopher.

Konan
A form of Conan found in Brittany.

Kyle
This may derive from the Gaelic for 'church' and is most frequently found in Scotland.

Kynon
This variation of Conan is to be found in Cornwall and Wales.

L ~ Boys

Labraid
In the old myths he was ruler of the kingdom of the immortal gods.

Lacey
The name of a powerful Irish family in the Middle Ages, which originally came from a French place name.

Lachlan
A Scottish name meaning 'from the land of the lochs', it was brought to Britain by the Vikings.

Ladra
One of the first men in the Celtic creation myth.

Lagman
A Manx name that means 'man of the law'.

Lancelot
One of the best-known Celtic names, he was a Knight of the Round Table and the lover of Guinevere, King Arthur's queen.
OTHER FORMS: Lance, Launcelot.

Lann
Derived from the Gaelic for 'sword'.

Lanval
A Knight of the Round Table who bragged about being married to a goddess, but when her secret was discovered she left him and went back to her own world.

Laoghaire
The name of an ancient Irish warrior and also a place name in Ireland.

Latharn
The founder of one of the early Scottish kingdoms. The name is derived from the Gaelic word for 'fox'.

Laurys
A Manx name that means 'crowned with laurels'.

Lear
This means 'sea' and is the name given by Shakespeare to the tragic king whose daughters betrayed him.

Lennan
Derived from the Irish Gaelic for 'meadow'.

Lennon
Possibly a variation of Lennan, but used as a first name in honour of the Beatle, John Lennon.

Lennox
Originally a Scottish surname meaning 'elm grove', this is now a popular first name due to the heavyweight boxer, Lennox Lewis.

Leslie
Taken from the surname of the Scots clan who were earls of Rothe.
SHORT FORM: Les.

Liag
A Manx name that means 'doctor'.

Liam
The Irish version of William, this came to the British Isles with the Normans in the form of Guillaume.

Lir
This name means 'sea' and he was the father of a sea god.

Llasar
The husband of Cymidea.

Lleu
Lleu Llaw was a Celtic god of the sun and his name means 'light'.

Lleufer
This Welsh name has the meaning 'splendour' or 'light'.

Llew
This can be a short version of Llewellyn or the name of a Celtic sun god.

Llewellyn
The name of two great Welsh princes, this is derived from the Welsh for 'lion'.
OTHER FORMS: Fluellen, Leoline, Llew, Llywelyn, Lyn.

Lloyd
This is a first name as well as a surname and means 'grey' in Welsh.
OTHER FORMS: Floyd, Loy, Loyd.

Lludd
The name of a sky god.

Lly
The name of a sea god.

Lóch
This old Celtic name means 'radiant'.

Lochinvar
This romantic name, used by Sir Walter Scott in his famous poem, implies a Viking from Inver.

Lochlan
A name that means 'Viking' and is therefore suitable for boys with red or blond hair.
OTHER FORMS: Lochie, Lochlin, Loghlan, Lolan.

Loegaire
In the sagas he was married to an immortal woman who gave him a magic horse on which to visit his own world, but when he got there everyone was dead as centuries had passed, and he too died as soon as his foot touched the ground.

Loez
One of the Breton forms of Louis.

Logan
Originally a Scottish place name and a surname, this probably comes from the Gaelic for 'hollow'. James H. Logan gave his name to the loganberry when he crossed a blackberry with a raspberry to create a new fruit.

Loic
A form of Louis found in Brittany.
OTHER FORM: Loig.

Lonan
The name of a saint from the Isle of Man who has a church dedicated to him.

Lorcan
Deriving from the Gaelic word that means 'fierce', this name was that of a 12th-century archbishop of Dublin.

Lorn
This Scottish name comes from the Gaelic for 'fox'.

Lorne
Derived from the Scottish place name, this can be used for girls as well as boys.

Lovocat
There is a record of a sixth-century Breton priest of this name.

Lucas
A Manx name that means 'grove'.

Lugaid
One of the High Kings of old Ireland who was reputed to have two red stripes dividing his body into three parts.

Luger

A bishop who founded a church at Rooskey in Ireland.

Lugh

One of the most powerful Celtic gods, he was the god of the sun and his name means 'shining one'.

Lughaidh

This name comes from Lugh and means 'shining one'. In the early sagas he fought and killed the great Cúchulainn.

Lulac

The king of Scotland who succeeded Macbeth to the throne.

Luthais

The Gaelic form of Lewis.

Lynfar

A Welsh name meaning 'lake'.

M ~ Boys

Mabon
The Celtic god of youth, altars to him were scattered throughout Europe.

Mac
Meaning 'son of', this is the first part of many Celtic names but is now sometimes used on its own.

Macaulay
This Scottish transferred surname means 'son of the phantom'.

Maccus
Reputed to be the name of a legendary king from the Isle of Man.

Macdonald
The name of a Scottish clan, this is used as a first name in Scotland.

Mackenzie
This comes from the Scots surname, meaning 'son of Coinneach'.
SHORT FORM: Mack.

Macsen
The Welsh equivalent of Magnus.

Maddox
From the Welsh for 'fortunate', this is the name given to her son by the film star Angelina Jolie.

Madeg
The Breton form of Madog.

Madern
The name of a Cornish saint and a place name, Madron, in Cornwall.

Madoc
Saint Madoc was a seventh-century Irish monk renowned for his piety. The name is derived from the Welsh for 'generous'.

Madog
A pet form of the Irish Aodh, which means 'fire'.
OTHER FORM: Madeg.

Mael

The founder of the Servants of God religious order in the eighth century.

Magnus

There was an 11th-century Earl of Orkney with this name.
OTHER FORMS: Manus, Maxen.

Maighnenn

The name of an early abbot of Kilmainham.

Maine

The name of all seven sons of Queen Medb and King Ailill.

Malcolm

The name of four Scottish kings, this comes from the Gaelic meaning 'follower of Saint Columb'.
OTHER FORMS: Colum, Mal.

Malise

Meaning 'servant of Jesus', this was formerly used by various earls of Strathearn.
OTHER FORM: Maoilios.

Malmore

A Manx version of Miles.

Malo

A Breton saint after whom the port of St Malo in Brittany is thought to be named.

Malooney

A Manx name meaning 'servant of the church'.

Manannán

The Celtic sea god and the name of the first king of the Isle of Man.
OTHER FORM: Manawydan.

Manas

Saint Manas founded Kirkwall Cathedral in Orkney.

Mangan

Derived from the Gaelic for 'having abundant hair'.

Maodez

A Breton version of Mawes.

Maol

The name of some of the early Scottish kings.

Maolíosa

This means 'disciple of Jesus' and can be used for both boys and girls.

Marcán

A historical Celtic ruler whose name means 'horse'.

Marcus

A Manx name that means 'hammer'.
OTHER FORM: Markys.

Maredudd

An old Welsh form of Meredith.

Margh

The Cornish version of Mark, this means 'horse'.

Mark

The anglicised version of Margh. He was the king of Cornwall who married Iseult, who then fell in love with Tristan, after which there followed the well-known tale of separation and woe.
OTHER FORMS: Margh, Marrec.

Marmaduke

Derived from the Irish Gaelic for 'follower of Madoc'.
SHORT FORM: Duke.

Marrec

This Cornish name, which means 'horseman', is one of the variations of Mark.

Martainn

The Gaelic form of Martin.

Martyn

A saint's name that means 'martial'.

Masek

The Cornish form of the Welsh name Madoc, this means 'fortunate'.

Massen

The name of a Cornish king.

Mata

A Gaelic pet form of Matthew.

Math

A wise and mighty Welsh king who was reputed to need a virgin to hold his feet in her lap in order to be happy.

Mawes

The Irish Saint Mawes gave his name to the town in Cornwall.
OTHER FORMS: Maodez, Maudez, Modez.

Mawgan

A sixth-century Cornish saint.

Maxen

This name means 'great' and is a Welsh form of Magnus.

Maxwell

A Scottish surname that means 'Maccus's stream'.

SHORT FORM: Max.

Mayl

A Manx name that means 'like God'.

Mechi

Son of The Morrigan, he had three hearts, all of which contained a serpent.

Meilyr

This Welsh name comes from the words 'iron' and 'man'.

Mel

The name of an early bishop of Ardagh.

Melan

The name of an obscure Celtic saint who was revered in Cornwall.

OTHER FORM: Mellanus.

Melor

The patron saint of Mylor in Cornwall, although it is probable that he came from Brittany.

OTHER FORM: Melorus.

Melville

Originally the name of a Scottish town, this was used as a surname and then a first name.

OTHER FORM: Melvin.

Meredith

From the Welsh for 'great chief'.

OTHER FORMS: Meredydd, Meriadeg, Merry.

Meredydd

An old Welsh form of Meredith.

Meriadeg

A Breton version of Meredith.

OTHER FORM: Meriadoc.

Meriadoc

A variation of Meriadeg found mainly in Wales.

Meriasek

The name of a Cornish saint.

Merlene

A variation of Merlin.

Merlin

The legendary wise man, or magician, who was King Arthur's mentor and advisor. He was reputed to be the son of an incubus and a nun.

OTHER FORMS: Marlin, Merlyn, Merle, Merlene.

Mervyn

From the Welsh for 'sea fort'.
OTHER FORMS: Marvin, Mervin.

Meryn

An old Cornish name of uncertain meaning.

Meurig

The Welsh form of Maurice.

Miach

The brother of Airmid in Irish legends and son of the god of medicine, Diancecht. He discovered how to replace missing limbs with real flesh and blood arms or legs.

Miall

A Manx name meaning 'like God'.

Mian

A Manx name meaning 'good'.

Miar

A Welsh name of uncertain meaning.

Michéal

The Gaelic version of Michael.

Michel

A Manx form of Michael.

Midir

The name of a god who was called 'the proud'.

Mikael

A form of Michael found in Brittany.

Milo

An Irish form of Miles.

Mingus

A variation of Angus.

Móen

A legendary hero who was struck dumb when he was a child but was cured by the love of his wife Moriath.

Moirreach

The Gaelic version of Murray.

Mold

A Manx name meaning 'earth born'.

Moling

In sixth-century Ireland he was a religious man who founded the church of St Mullins.

Mongán

The name of an early ruler in Welsh myths.

Mongfhinn
He was a king of Munster in Irish myths.

Monier
A Manx name meaning 'mountain'.

Monroe
Taken from the Scottish surname, this probably originated in Ireland.
OTHER FORM: Munro.

Moran
This first name is found in Brittany as well as being a transferred surname in Ireland.
OTHER FORM: Moren.

Morcant
A Welsh form of Morgan.

Mordred
The name of a legendary Knight of the Round Table who rebelled against King Arthur.

More
A Manx name meaning 'illustrious'.

Morgan
A transferred Irish or Welsh surname meaning 'bright' or 'sea-born'.
OTHER FORMS: Morcant, Morien.

Moris
A Manx name meaning 'dark-coloured'.

Morvan
A Breton form of Marvin.
OTHER FORM: Morven.

Morven
A variation of Morvan, which may be derived from the Gaelic for 'great' and 'fair-haired'.

Mugint
He came from Ireland and opened a university in Scotland where there were female as well as male students.

Muir
A transferred Scottish surname that is derived from 'moor'.

Muirchertach
A name borne by several medieval Irish kings.

Muireachadh
Derived from the Gaelic meaning 'warrior from the sea'.

Muirinn
From the Irish Gaelic for 'white as the sea'.

Muiris

The source of the 'Song of Dermot and the Earl', a 14th-century poem about the life of King Diarmait.

Mungo

Saint Kentigern, who was Bishop of Glasgow, was known as Saint Mungo. The name comes from the Gaelic for 'beloved' and was borne by the Scottish explorer Mungo Park, who traced the source of the River Niger.
OTHER FORM: Mungan.

Murchadh

This means 'sea warrior' in Gaelic and was the name of the eldest son of Brian Boru.
OTHER FORM: Murrough.

Murdagh

A variation of Murghad.

Murdoch

A variation of Murtaugh that is mainly found in Scotland.
OTHER FORM: Murdo.

Murghad

This Manx name can be traced back to the early 16th century on the Isle of Man.
OTHER FORM: Murdagh.

Murphy

Derived from the Gaelic for 'sea battle' and used both as a surname and a first name.

Murray

This clan name comes from Scotland and is probably related to the district of Moray, which got its name from the Celtic for 'settlement by the sea'.
OTHER FORMS: Moirreach, Moray, Murrie.

Murtaugh

An old Gaelic name meaning 'sea battle'.
OTHER FORM: Murdoch.

Myghal

A Cornish version of Michael.

Mylor

A saint revered by the Celts whose name may mean 'man of iron'.

Myrddin

The Welsh version of Merlin, the magician, this means 'sea fort'.

N ~ Boys

Nadelek
A Cornish name from the word for 'Christmas'.

Nairn
From the Gaelic for 'one who lives by the alder tree'.

Naoise
A young man in the old legends with whom Deirdre of the Sorrows falls in love.
OTHER FORMS: Naoisi, Nyse.

Nechtan
A name from the Irish legends, his wife Boann are forbidden nuts from the tree by the fountain of knowledge, which overflowed and ran after her and became the River Boyne.

Nedeleg
This Breton name means 'Christmas' and thus is the equivalent of Noel.

Neil
Taken from the Gaelic for 'cloud'.
OTHER FORMS: Neal, Nyle.

Nellyn
A Manx name meaning 'little champion'.

Nelson
This means 'champion's son', although most people associate it with the famous admiral of the same name.

Nemed
The leader of the third invasion of Ireland.

Nessan
This was the name of several Irish saints and may mean 'stoat'.

Nevan
This is connected to the Gaelic for 'holy' or 'saint'.

Neven
There is a feast day in Brittany in honour of Saint Neven.

Nevyn
A Manx name that means 'saint'.

Neythen

A Cornish saint who, in the legends, had his head cut off while trying to convert some robbers. He calmly picked it up and walked back to his hut.

Niall

The name of a famous Irish king who was called Niall of the Nine Hostages; it means 'champion' in Gaelic.
OTHER FORMS: Nel, Nele.

Nicca

The Cornish nickname for Nicholas.

Ninean

A Gaelic version of Ninian.

Ninian

The name of a fifth-century saint who converted the Picts in Scotland to Christianity.
OTHER FORMS: Nennian, Ninean, Ninidh, Ninn.

Ninn

A form of Ninian found in Brittany.

Niocal

A Gaelic version of Nicholas.

Nissien

The twin brother of Efnissien, who was war-like, but Nissien only wanted everyone to be at peace.

Nuada

An Irish king of the gods who had his right hand cut off in battle, which was first replaced by a silver hand and then by a real flesh and blood hand made by Miach.

Nudd

A Celtic god of the sky and clouds.

Nwyfre

The god of space.

Nye

A short form of Aneurin.

Nyle

An Irish version of Neil.

Nynniaw

The name of an old Welsh god.

O ~ Boys

Odairr
A royal Manx name meaning 'twilight sword'.

Odhran
Derived from the Gaelic for 'dark-haired'.
OTHER FORM: Odran.

Oengus
He wrote a famous martyrology in the ninth century, entitled *Félire*.

Ogilvy
The name of an old Scottish clan, this means 'high plain' in Gaelic.

Ogma
The Celtic god of eloquence.

Oileabhéar
The Irish equivalent of Oliver.

Oisín
From the Gaelic, 'little deer'; he was the son of the legendary Finn Mac Cool.
OTHER FORMS: Osheen, Oshin.

Okerfair
A Manx name meaning 'our fair one'.

Olaf
A royal name in the Isle of Man, this means 'of the gods'.
OTHER FORM: Olave.

Olc
A name meaning 'evil'.

Oliver
Originally a Norman name that meant 'olive tree', it was adopted by the Celts.
OTHER FORM: Oileabhéar.

Onllwyn
This Welsh name comes from the name of a village in Glamorgan and means 'ash grove'.

Oran
The name of an Irish saint in the sixth century, this comes from the Gaelic for 'pale-skinned'.

Orry

This comes from the Isle of Man with the meaning of 'man from the Orient'.
OTHER FORM: Orrey.

Oscar

The name of Oisín's son in the Fenian sagas, this means 'beloved of deer'.
OTHER FORMS: Osgar, Osgur, Ossie, Ozzie.

Oshin

A Manx form of Oisín.

Ossian

A Scottish form of Oisín used in the 18th-century *The Poems of Ossian,* which led to a great interest in Celtic history and art.

Ottar

A royal name on the Isle of Man that means 'twilight sword'.
OTHER FORM: Oter.

Owain

The original Owain was supposed to be the ancestor of the kings of South Wales.
OTHER FORM: Owayne.

Owen

A very popular Welsh name. Owen or Owain Glendower headed an uprising against the English in the 15th century.

Ownie

Connected to the Irish Gaelic for 'green'.
OTHER FORM: Owny.

P ~ Boys

Padarn
The name of a sixth-century Breton saint, whose saint's day is still celebrated in Brittany.
OTHER FORM: Patern.

Padeen
A Manx name meaning 'little Patrick'.

Padern
The name of an early Cornish chieftain.
OTHER FORM: Patern.

Pádraig
The Celtic form of Patrick.
OTHER FORMS: Padrig, Padruig, Páid, Páidín.

Paric
A Manx name meaning 'patrician' or 'noble'.
OTHER FORM: Peric.

Parlan
Possibly meaning 'waves of the sea', this is the origin of surnames such as Macfarlane.

Parthalán
The name of an early settler in Ireland who cut down much of the forested area in the centre of the country so that the land could be farmed.
OTHER FORMS: Parthalon, Partlan.

Pasco
A Cornish name from the word for Easter that was popular up until the 17th century.

Patern
A variation of Padern.

Paton
A Manx diminutive of Patrick.
OTHER FORM: Pattoone.

Patrick
The legendary patron saint of Ireland who was reputed to have eradicated all the snakes from the island and converted the inhabitants to Christianity.
OTHER FORMS: Paddy, Pádraig, Pat, Paton, Patric, Patryk, Paudeen, Rick.

Pawly
This variation of Paul comes from Cornwall.

Payl
A Manx version of Paul.

Peadar
An Irish form of Peter.

Pearce
An Irish version of Piers.
OTHER FORMS: Pearse, Pierce.

Peddyr
A Manx name meaning 'rock'.

Peder
A Cornish form of Peter.

Pedr
This form of Peter is found in Wales.

Pencast
This name comes from the Cornish word for Pentecost.

Penwyn
In Welsh this means 'white head'.

Percival
The name of one of the legendary Knights of the Round Table who completed his quest for the Holy Grail.

Peredur
A seventh son, who therefore had supernatural powers, he was a hero in the Arthurian legends.

Perig
A Breton form of Piers.
SHORT FORM: Per.

Petroc
The patron saint of miners in Cornwall who founded a monastery in Padstow in the sixth century.
OTHER FORM: Petroke.

Petrog
A Cornish name derived from the word for 'rock'.

Phelan
An old Irish name derived from the Gaelic for 'wolf'.

Phelim
An ancient Irish name borne by three kings of Munster and by a 16th-century warrior who defeated the English in the battle of Glenmalure.
OTHER FORM: Phelimy.

Piers

Originally this name, which is derived from the word for 'rock', came from Normandy to Ireland.

OTHER FORMS: Pearce, Perig, Piaras.

Pilib

The name of a Celtic poet who came from Sligo in Ireland.

Piran

Saint Piran was an Irish monk who founded a monastery in Cornwall. The Cornish flag has the cross of Saint Piran on it.

OTHER FORMS: Peran, Perran.

Plebig

One of the sons of the early Celtic ruler, Elen.

Pól

The Gaelic version of Paul.

Powell

A transferred surname, this comes from the Welsh for 'son of Hywel'.

Price

A Welsh surname derived from 'ap (son of) Rhys', also used as a first name.

OTHER FORM: Pryce.

Proinsias

An Irish form of Francis, which originally meant 'man from France'.

Pryderi

A seeker of a magic bowl in the Welsh myths, a precursor of the Holy Grail stories.

Pwyll

A lord of Dyfed in Welsh myths, the name means 'prudence'.

Q ~ Boys

Queran
A variation of Ciarán.

Quigley
Possibly derives from the Gaelic words meaning 'of beautiful shape'.

Quillan
Probably from the Gaelic for 'beautiful shape'.
OTHER FORMS: Quill, Quinlan, Quinlevan.

Quinn
Probably a variation of Conn, which means 'intelligent'.

Quinton
Saint Quinton was the patron saint of Kirkmahoe in Scotland.
OTHER FORM: Quentin.

Quisten
A Manx name possibly derived from the word for 'solicitude'.

R ~ Boys

Rab
A Scottish short form of Robert.

Rabbie
The name of the Scottish poet Robert Burns is often affectionately shortened to Rabbie.

Rafferty
A transferred surname, this derives from the Gaelic for 'rich' or 'prosperous'.

Raghallaigh
This transferred surname is taken from the Gaelic for 'brave, courageous'.

Raghnall
A Scottish version of Ronald.

Raibert
A Scottish form of Robert.

Ramsay
The name of a place and a clan in Scotland, known because of the politician Ramsay MacDonald.

Ramsey
The name of a place in the Isle of Man, which means 'raven's island' or 'ram's island'.

Ranald
A Scottish form of Ronald.

Randal
A very old ballad in Scotland is named after Lord Randal, and the name may mean 'ruler's advice'.
OTHER FORM: Ranulf.

Reagan
This transferred surname means either 'king' or 'impulsive'.
OTHER FORM: Regan.

Reaman
An Irish name derived from the Gaelic for 'counsellor'.
OTHER FORM: Reamon.

Redmond
The Irish version of Raymond and the name of a renowned 17th-century highwayman.

Reece

Derived from the Welsh for 'passion'.
OTHER FORM: Rees.

Reginald

Two bishops and two kings of the Isle of Man bore this name.

Reid

Meaning 'red' or 'redhead', this is a transferred surname.

Reilly

A very popular Irish surname that is sometimes used as a first name.
OTHER FORM: Riley.

Reith

A transferred surname that possibly comes from the Gaelic for 'grace'.

Rewan

An early Cornish bishop and saint.

Reynold

The name of two kings of the Isle of Man.

Rhain

This Welsh name is derived from the word for 'lance'.

Rhodri

May derive from the Welsh for 'wheel'. A Welsh chieftain bore the name in the ninth century.

Rhydach

This Cornish name probably derives from a Celtic place name meaning 'infertile land'.
OTHER FORMS: Rhydoch, Riddock.

Rhydderch

A Welsh name that means 'reddish brown'.

Rhydwyn

This Welsh name means 'white ford'.

Rhys

The son of Gwenllian and Gruffydd, he was the organiser of the first known Welsh eisteddfod in 1176.
OTHER FORM: Rhett.

Rick

A short form of Patrick.

Ridseard

A Gaelic version of Richard.

Rigard

A Manx form of Richard.

Riobard

This Irish name is derived from the Gaelic for 'fame' and is also thought of as the Irish form of Robert.
OTHER FORM: Riobart.

Riordan

This Irish name means 'royal poet'.
OTHER FORM: Rearden.

Roarke

This Irish name is derived from the Gaelic for 'famous ruler'.
OTHER FORMS: Rorke, Rourke, Ruark.

Rob

A short form of Roban and Robart, amongst others.

Robaidh

A Gaelic variation of Robin.

Roban

One of the Gaelic versions of Robin.
SHORT FORM: Rob.

Robart

A Manx form of Robert.
SHORT FORM: Rob.

Robyn

A Manx name meaning 'little Robert'.

Roc

An Irish myth has it that Roc was turned into a frog and could only say his name, therefore all frogs make the sound 'Roc, Roc'.
OTHER FORM: Rocky.

Rochad

A warrior of the elite guard of the ancient kings of Ulster.

Roden

A transferred surname that comes from the Gaelic for 'strong'.

Roderick

From the Gaelic for 'strong'.
OTHER FORMS: Roddy, Rody.

Rodhlann

The name Roland was brought to Ireland by the Normans and this is the Irish version of the name.

Rogan

One of the Irish names derived from the Gaelic for 'red-haired'.

Roibeard

This Irish version of Robert comes from the Gaelic for 'bright fame'.
OTHER FORM: Roibeart.

Roidh

A Gaelic version of Roy.

Romney

This may be derived from the Gaelic for 'curving river'.

Ronan

Several saints bore this name, which means 'little seal'.

Rooney

A transferred surname that means 'little redhead', this is gaining popularity due to the footballer, Wayne Rooney.

Rory

A very popular name in Ireland that means 'redhead'.

Ross

The name of a Scottish clan, which comes from the Gaelic for 'peninsula'.
OTHER FORM: Ros.

Rowan

The name of several Irish saints and of a tree with red berries, this means 'little redhead'.
OTHER FORMS: Rowen, Rowie, Rowney.

Roy

A Scottish name taken from the Gaelic for 'red'.
OTHER FORM: Roidh.

Ruadhan

Son of the goddess Brigid, he was a great warrior.

Ruadhrí

This may come from the Gaelic for 'red-haired' or for 'red king'.

Ruan

The name of a Cornish saint.

Ruaraidh

The name of a king of Connacht who recognised Henry II as his sovereign.

Ruari

From the Gaelic for 'red-haired'.

Ruiseart

A Gaelic version of Richard.

Rumo

The name of a Cornish bishop who was put to death and became a martyr for his Christian belief.
OTHER FORM: Rumon.

Rumund

A Manx form of Raymond.

Ryan

Possibly from the Gaelic meaning 'little king'.

OTHER FORMS: Rian, Ryne.

Rydderch

A name derived from the Welsh for 'reddish brown'.

Ryol

The name of a king in an early Cornish play.

S ~ Boys

Sandaidh
A Gaelic version of Sandy.

Sandulf
A Manx name reputed to mean 'sand wolf'.

Sandy
A short form of Alastair.
OTHER FORMS: Sandaidh, Saunder.

Saoirse
This name is used for girls as well as boys and means 'freedom'.

Saunder
A Gaelic version of Sandy.

Sayer
An anglicised form of the Gaelic for 'craftsman'.

Scanlan
More usually found as a surname, this is thought to mean 'attractive'.
OTHER FORM: Scanlon.

Sceolan
In the myths he was a hound as well as a man and his name means 'fleet of foot'.

Scoithíne
The name of an early saint, renowned for his austerity.

Scott
An Irish tribe called the Scotti settled in Scotland in the sixth century so this name means 'person from Scotland'.

Seamas
A Scottish form of James.

Seamus
An Irish form of James.
OTHER FORMS: Hamish, Seumas, Shamus.

Seán
The Celtic version of John, this means 'God's gracious gift'.
OTHER FORMS: Shane, Shantaigh, Shaun.

Seanan

A traditional Irish name from the Gaelic for 'old' or 'venerable'.

Seanchán

The name of an early Irish poet.

Seithynin

A mythical drunkard who receives his just deserts when he ravishes a young girl.

Selevan

The name of an early Cornish saint.

Semias

A legendary wise man whose cooking pot was full of wisdom. Whoever partook of it could know not only what would happen in the future but also what had happened in the past.

Senán

The name of a sixth-century Irish saint. OTHER FORM: Sionán.

Sencha

A legendary chief judge in Ireland.

Seoras

A Gaelic version of George.

Seosamh

The Irish form of Joseph.

Setanta

This was the original name of Cúchulainn.

Seucha

In the Celtic tradition this was the name of a supremely wise man.

Sezni

A Breton form of Senan, a name that implies wisdom.

Shane

A northern Irish variation of Seán.

Shanley

A transferred Irish surname that means 'venerable warrior'.

Shannon

Related to the Gaelic for 'old' and 'wise' and is also the name of the longest river in Ireland.

Shantaigh

Originally a pet form of Seán, this is also used in its own right.

Sharry

A Manx name meaning 'God's peace'.

Shaun

A southern Irish form of Seán. OTHER FORMS: Shaughan, Shawn.

Shaw
There is a Scottish clan with this name and it is also used in Ireland, possibly as a form of Shea.

Shea
This transferred surname has the meaning 'hawk-like'.

Sheridan
Also a surname, this originally derived from Gaelic but its meaning is unknown.

Sholto
From the Gaelic 'sower', this is one of the names of the Scottish Douglas family.

Sigurd
Originally a Scandinavian name that means 'victorious'.

Sigvald
A Manx name of Scandinavian origin.

Sim
A Gaelic version of Simon.

Sinclair
A Scottish name that comes from Saint Claire, which means 'holy light'.

Sion
The Welsh form of John.

Sithny
This comes from the Celtic word for 'peace' and is the name of a Cornish saint to whose well sick dogs are taken on his feast day.

Skelly
From the Gaelic for 'story-teller'.

Somhairle
A name borne by the chieftain of Argyll in the 12th century, this is also found in Ireland and the Isle of Man.
OTHER FORMS: Somerled, Sorley, Summerlad.

Steafan
A Gaelic version of Stephen.

Steffan
A Welsh form of Stephen.

Stewart
The original bearer of this name was the High Steward of Scotland.

Stiubhart
A Gaelic version of Stuart.

Stiurt

A Manx form of Stuart.

Stoill

A Manx name meaning 'with a will'.

Strachan

A transferred Scottish surname that means 'poet'.

Strahan

From the Gaelic for 'poet' or 'wise man'.

Struan

A Scottish name that may be derived from the Gaelic for 'stream'.

Struther

From the Gaelic name meaning 'stream'.

Stuart

The name of many kings of Scotland, this means 'chief of the royal household'.
OTHER FORMS: Stiubhart, Stiurt.

Sucat

From the Gaelic 'warrior', this was Saint Patrick's baptismal name.

Suibhne

Many Irish kings and saints bore this name.

Sulian

A Breton form of Julian.

Sulien

This Welsh name is reputed to mean 'summer child'.

Sullivan

A transferred surname derived from the Gaelic for 'keen-eyed'.

Sweeney

From the Gaelic meaning 'little hero', this name has unfortunate connotations such as the murderous barber Sweeney Todd.

Syme

A Scottish form of Simon.

T ~ Boys

Tadhg
A Scottish or Irish name meaning 'poet' or 'philosopher'.

Tafydd
A variation of the Welsh Dafydd.

Talan
An old Cornish and Breton name.

Talek
This Cornish name means 'big-browed'.

Taliesin
From the Welsh 'shining brow', it was the name of a sixth-century Welsh poet.

Tanguy
This Breton saint has a feast day on 16 November.

Tangwyn
A Welsh name that means 'blessed peace'.

Tarlach
A short form of an Irish High King's name.

Tasgall
An old Scottish Gaelic name.

Tavish
A Scottish version of Thomas.
OTHER FORM: Tam.

Tearlach
In Scotland this name was used for those called Charles, particularly for Bonnie Prince Charlie.

Teilo
The name of an early Welsh saint who was reputed to perform miracles.

Teimhnín
The name of two saints, this comes from a Gaelic word for 'dark'.

Terence

Sometimes spelt with a double 'r', this is an Irish name that probably means 'polished'.

OTHER FORM: Torrance.

Tewdrig

A Cornish ruler who put to death Celtic missionaries who were trying to convert his people to Christianity.

Tewdwr

A Welsh variant spelling of Tudor.

Thane

The name for a clan chief in Scotland.

Thomase

A traditional Manx form of Thomas.

Thorfin

This is a royal Manx name meaning 'Thor's finder'.

OTHER FORM: Thorryn.

Thorkell

A Manx name meaning 'Thor's holy vessel'.

OTHER FORM: Thorgil.

Thorleot

A Manx name meaning 'Thor's people'.

Thorlief

A Manx name meaning 'left by Thor'.

Thorman

A Manx name meaning 'Thor's man'.

Thormod

A Manx name meaning 'Thor's wrath'.

OTHER FORM: Thormot.

Thorulf

A Manx name meaning 'Thor's wolf'.

Thurstan

A Manx name meaning 'Thor's stone'.

Tiernan

From the Gaelic word that means 'lord'.

Tierney

The name of a sixth-century Irish saint who was baptised by Saint Brigid.

Tighearnach

In sixth-century Ireland there was a bishop of this name.

Tomas

The Gaelic version of Thomas.

Tón

An Irish short form of Anthony.

Torcall
The Gaelic equivalent of Torquil.

Torin
The Irish Gaelic for 'chief'.

Tormod
The Gaelic equivalent of Norman.

Tostig
A Welsh name meaning 'pointed'.

Trahaearn
From the Welsh, meaning 'strong as iron', this was the name of an 11th-century king of Gwynedd.
OTHER FORM: Trahern.

Trefor
The Welsh form of Trevor.

Tremaine
From the Cornish place name meaning 'the house on the rock'.
OTHER FORM: Tremayne.

Trent
The name of a river, which means 'one who lives by a stream'.

Trevedic
This Cornish name is derived from the word for 'country dweller'.

Trevelyan
A transferred Cornish surname meaning 'home of the bright one'.

Trevor
From the Welsh meaning 'large homestead', this is also found as a surname.
OTHER FORMS: Trefor, Trev, Trevon.

Tristan
An old Celtic name borne by the tragic romantic hero who loved Iseult or Isolde.
OTHER FORMS: Tristram, Tristran.

Tuathal
Derived from the Irish Gaelic meaning 'people's leader'.
OTHER FORMS: Tole, Tully.

Tudor
Possibly a version of Theodore, this Welsh name became the surname of the British royal family in the 15th century.

Tudur
From the Welsh meaning 'ruler of the tribe'.

Tugdual
The name of a Breton saint.

Turlough

An Irish name that may be derived from the Gaelic for 'instigator'.

OTHER FORMS: Thurloe, Turloch, Thurlow, Turlow.

Tynam

From the Gaelic for 'dark' or 'grey'.

SHORT FORM: Ty.

Tyree

An Irish name taken from County Tyrone.

Tyrone

From the name of an Irish county.

U ~ Boys

Uaithne
Derived from the Gaelic for 'green' or 'verdant'.
OTHER FORM: Uaine.

Uallas
The Gaelic version of Wallace.

Uilliam
The Gaelic version of William.

Uinseann
The Irish equivalent of Vincent.

Uisdean
A Gaelic equivalent of Hugh.

Ultán
An Irish missionary who became abbot of Nivelles in the seventh century.

Urchurdan
The Scottish Gaelic version of Urquhart.

Urien
Possibly derived from the Welsh for 'town'.
OTHER FORM: Urian.

Urmen
A Manx name that means 'warrior'.

Urmonek
A ninth-century Breton monk who wrote a book called *Life of St Pol de Léon*.

Urquhart
The name of a Scottish clan, one of whose chiefs was reputed to have died laughing in 1660.
OTHER FORM: Urchurdan.

Usna
An Ulster chieftain, one of whose sons was married to the famous Deirdre.

Uthr
Uthr Pendragon was the father of King Arthur in the Arthurian legends.

V ~ Boys

Vaughan
This transferred surname is derived from the Welsh for 'small'.
OTHER FORMS: Vaughn, Vychan.

Vaundie
A Manx name meaning 'a bond'.

Vause
A 16th-century Manx name meaning 'noble'.

Venutius
A seventh-century British chieftain.

Vergobret
Derived from the Celtic words for 'effective' and 'judgement', this was the name of early law-givers.

Viking
A Manx name meaning 'sea rover'.

Viridomar
The name of a Celtic king in 222 BC.

Visant
A Breton version of Vincent.

Vivian
The male form of Vivien.

Vortigern
A High King of Britain whose name means 'overlord'.

Vychan
A Welsh version of Vaughan.

W ~ Boys

Wallace

A name derived from the word meaning 'foreigner', it was used by the Scots to describe the Celts. The 13th-century William Wallace was known as Braveheart and his name is extremely well known due to the film of that name.

OTHER FORMS: Uallas, Wallis, Walsh, Welch, Welsh.

Waylon

Reputed to be a Celtic name meaning 'son of the wolf'.

OTHER FORM: Weylin.

Wella

A Cornish form of William.

Winwaloe

A variation of Guénole, who was a sixth-century abbot of the monastery of Landévennec in Brittany.

Withell

This Cornish name comes from the word for 'lion'.

Wrmonec

A ninth-century Breton monk at the monastery of Landévennec in Brittany.

Wyllow

The name of a sixth-century Cornish saint to whom the church at Lanteglos is dedicated.

Wyn

From the Welsh for 'white' or 'blessed'.

OTHER FORM: Wynne.

Wynford

Probably a variation of Gwynfor.

Y, Z ~ Boys

Yann
The name of a 14th-century king of Brittany, this is a popular Cornish and Breton name.

Yestin
The Welsh and Cornish form of Justin.

Ynyr
A traditional Welsh name, possibly meaning 'honour'.

Yollan
An alternative spelling of Iollan.
OTHER FORM: Yolland.

Yorath
A variation of Iorweth.

Yorwin
From the Gaelic for 'pure and handsome lord'.

Ysaig
A Manx form of Isaac.

Ythel
The name of a king of Britanny and of Cornwall.

Yvar
An old Manx form of Ivor.
OTHER FORMS: Yveno, Yvor.

Yveno
A Manx variation of Yvar.

Yvon
A Manx form of John.

Ywain
A Welsh name that means 'young warrior'.

Zenan
A Cornish name meaning 'old and wise'.
OTHER FORM: Zenon.

Zethar
A Cornish name meaning 'seagull'.

40,001 Best Baby Names
Diane Stafford
With a comprehensive, easy-to-use alphabetical listing of 40,001 baby names, plus fun, individualised lists, such as 'good names for race-car drivers', 'names for children who are handsome or beautiful', 'names for smart kids' and much more, this book is the essential resource for all parents-to-be.

Birth and Beyond
The ultimate guide to your pregnancy, your baby, your family
Dr Yehudi Gordon
Written by one of the world's leading obstetricians, this extraordinary book takes a totally fresh look at all aspects of life, through the nine months of pregnancy and the following nine of the baby's life. It is both a practical handbook for pregnancy, birth and the early months of a new baby's life, and an A-Z of health, acting as a superb source of reference for any new parent.

The New Contented Little Baby Book
The secret to calm and confident parenting
Gina Ford
Fully updated and including helpful input from clients, readers and mothers
who love her routines, this book gives you reassuring and practical advice that
works from Britain's number one childcare expert.

What to Expect When You're Breast-feeding...and What If You Can't?
'This book should be handed out with the first contraction.' Kate Beckinsale
Clare Byam-Cook
Fully revised and updated this guide covers all the information you could
possibly need to breast-feed your baby successfully, and gives practical,
sympathetic advice on how to feed your baby well if you can't.

Secrets of the Baby Whisperer
How to calm, connect and communicate with your baby
Tracy Hogg with Melinda Blau
Reassuring, down-to-earth and often flying in the face of conventional wisdom, this book promises parents not only a healthier, happier baby, but a more relaxed and happy household as well.

The Baby Development Test
A step-by-step guide to your baby's development from birth to 5 years
Dr Dorothy Einon
The only book that enables you to test your baby's physical, cognitive and social development.

☐ 40,001 Best Baby Names	9780091900007	£6.99
☐ Birth and Beyond	9780091856946	£20.00
☐ The New Contented Little Baby Book	9780091912697	£9.99
☐ What to Expect When You're Breast-feeding . . .	9780091906962	£8.99
☐ Secrets of the Baby Whisperer	9780091857028	£10.99
☐ The Baby Development Test	9780091910518	£7.99

FREE POSTAGE AND PACKING

Overseas customers allow £2.00 per paperback.

BY PHONE: 01624 677237

BY POST: Random House Books
c/o Bookpost, PO Box 29, Douglas
Isle of Man, IM99 1BQ

BY FAX: 01624 670923

BY EMAIL: bookshop@enterprise.net

Cheques (payable to Bookpost) and credit cards accepted.

Prices and availability subject to change without notice.
Allow 28 days for delivery.
When placing your order, please mention if you do not wish to receive any
additional information.

www.randomhouse.co.uk